PORSCHE 911
RED BOOK 1965-1999

Patrick C. Paternie

MBI Publishing Company

Acknowledgments

Special thanks to Jens Torner and Olaf Lang at Porsche AG and to Bob Carlson and Eleanor Smith at Porsche Cars North America for their assistance. Craig Stevenson, Ted Mumm, and Phil and Pat Van Buskirk also contributed to the research that went into this book.

First published in 2000 by MBI Publishing Company, 729 Prospect Avenue, PO Box 1, Osceola, WI 54020-0001 USA

MBI Publishing Company books are also available at discounts in bulk quantity for industrial or sales-promotional use. For details write to Special Sales Manager at Motorbooks International Wholesalers & Distributors, 729 Prospect Avenue, PO Box 1, Osceola, WI 54020-0001 USA.

Library of Congress Cataloging-in-Publication Data
Paternie, Patrick C.
        Porsche 911 red book 1965–1999 / Patrick Paternie.
              p. cm.
        Includes index.
        ISBN 0-7603-0723-7 (pbk. : alk. paper)
          1. Porsche 911 automobile—History. I. Title.
      TL215.P75 P3824   2000
      629.222'2'09—dc21   00-026958

On the front cover: Nothing says "Porsche" more than the sleek outline of a classic 911. Having evolved and survived for more than thirty-five years, today's Porsche 911 still embodies the classic look of this 1965 model. *David Newhardt*

On the back cover: The reason the Porsche 911 is the world's most recognizable car is that during its 30+ years of production, the shape of the car retained an essence of the original design. The family resemblance is easily recognized in this portrait of the 1984 Carrera (right) and its older sibling, a 1965 911 (left). *Porsche Werkfoto*

Edited by John Adams-Graf
Designed by LeAnn Kuhlmann
Printed in the United States of America

Contents

Introduction

Porsche 911 Red Book is designed to be a portable history and reference manual of the Porsche 911 from pre-production prototypes to 1999 production models. It is not intended to replace any of the excellent detailed history books that have been written about the 911 but to be a quick and handy way to study and evaluate the originality and authenticity of a particular car, especially if it is being considered for purchase. The book uses chassis and engine serial numbers to trace the 911's year-by-year production history along with color charts, interior appointments, options, and customer racing versions. Factory reference codes for engines and transmissions are also provided to assist in identifying any "parts swapping" that may have been done.

The book is divided into sections that group model years by production similarities. These sections represent major developmental changes in the 911's history, which are explained at the beginning of each section.

When inspecting a car, the chassis serial number, or VIN (Vehicle Identification Number), is the primary way to determine the correct year and model. On 1970 and newer 911s built for the United States, the VIN will appear on the driver's-side windshield post as well as on tags mounted to the door jamb and inside the trunk. Cars built before 1969 will only have the chassis number located inside the trunk.

Please note that Porsche has used several chassis serial numbering systems through the years. Numbers or letters were added to depict differences in engine type, body style, safety equipment, or the vehicle's intended country or market. In 1981, automakers around the world, including Porsche, adopted a 17-digit system that is still in use today. Refer to the notes below each year's production chart for the explanation of the serial number code for that year.

Because emissions, noise, and/or safety laws have varied between countries at times, Porsche has built cars that are specific to meeting those laws. This has been particularly the case for cars delivered to the United States and Canada. Cars not identified for a specific country are referred to as "Rest of the World" (RoW) models. The VIN will differentiate RoW models from U.S. cars, providing a means of identifying "gray market" imports or cars that may not meet U.S. laws. Purchasing one of these cars could lead to problems in terms of registration, insurability, and/or warranty claims.

Once a car's year and model have been determined to be correct using the VIN, check to see that the engine serial number falls within the proper range of numbers for that given year and model.

While every effort has been made to provide information that is as accurate and as detailed as possible given the scope of this book, not all information for every year was available. This was especially the case with optional equipment. Through the years, optional equipment in some countries was included as standard equipment in other countries. To obtain information for a specific car, it is recommended that Porsche be contacted directly. Other investigative means to determine authenticity should also be used, especially when purchasing rare or racing models. The Porsche Club of America should be able to provide referrals to experts regarding various models of the 911.

The author assumes no responsibility for any loss arising from the use of this book. Readers who have corrections or interesting additions should feel free to contact the author in care of MBI Publishing Company.

The 1964 911 was very similar to 1965–1966 models. Note the following: wipers parked to the right side of the windshield, auxiliary fog lamps, and 4.5-inch steel wheels with hubcaps.

Chapter One
1964–1967

The 911 can trace its roots back to sketches drawn up by Ferry Porsche's eldest son, Ferdinand Alexander "Butzi" Porsche, in August 1959. The flat-six, overhead cam engine that gave its project name to the car, Type 901, was largely the work of Hans Mezger and a young engineer named Ferdinand Piech. Ferry Porsche's influence on the 911 was his insistence on the continuance of the fastback shape of the 356 based on a longer, 2,200-millimeter wheelbase. It was also Ferry's decision to drop development of pushrod engines in favor of the overhead cam design.

The Porsche 901 made its world debut in September 1963 at the Frankfurt International Automobile Show. Prototype number 5, chassis 13 325, painted yellow with a non-operational mock-up of the 901 engine, was the car on display. This car continued to appear in auto shows until February 1964, when it was fitted with a working engine for traveling on sales demonstration tours to European dealerships. It was later used as a test mule until an accident led it to be scrapped in December 1965.

Of the original 13 prototypes built between 1962 and 1964, only one is believed to have survived. This sole survivor, number 7 with chassis 13 327, has been restored and is owned by a private collector in the United States.

Production of the 911 began in September 1964. This is known as the "0," or Zero, series. After the Paris auto show in October 1964, French automaker Peugeot claimed that it held the rights to all car model numbers with *zero* as the middle digit. Porsche elected to switch rather than fight French logic, and so on November 10, 1964, the 911 designation was born. For many years, however, internally the car was still known as the 901 with part numbers carrying the prefix 901. Technically, because production began before the official name change to 911, it can be said that there were 82 cars built as 901s. They may not be the first 82 chassis numbers though; it appears that early cars were produced out of the sequence indicated by their chassis numbers. Following the practice of shutting down the plant for summer vacation, production years for 911s, including the first one, end in July. The next model year begins the following August. The "0" series of cars was basically the same for the model years 1965 through 1967.

1965: The first 911 models reached the United States in February 1965, with a price tag of $6,500. Standard equipment included a five-speed synchromesh transmission, 2.0-liter 130-horsepower engine, ZF rack-and-pinion steering, 13-millimeter front anti-roll bar, four-wheel disc brakes, and 4.5Jx15 steel wheels with

The 1967 911S (Super) was the first 911 to have Fuchs alloy wheels; these were only 4.5 inches wide.

165HR15 tires. The transmission (Type 901) had a racing or "dogleg" shift pattern that had first gear to the left and down with reverse above it. A wood-rimmed steering wheel and matching trim on the dash were also standard equipment. Other standard features of the first-production 911s were the single-circuit hydraulic brake system, non-adjustable front suspension settings, and a single 45-amp battery. A ZF limited-slip differential was an option. Another option was a Webasto gasoline heater (P1018).

1966: The Porsche 912 was introduced. It mated the four-cylinder engine of the 356SC to the 911 body.

Weber carburetors replaced the Solex units during the production year, beginning in March 1966.

1967: 911S (Super) debuted offering a 160-horsepower 2.0-liter engine plus upgraded suspension, brakes, and wheels. The S package included 4.5Jx15 Fuchs alloy wheels, Koni shock absorbers, ventilated brake discs, front anti-roll bar increased to 15 millimeters plus the addition of a 16-millimeter rear bar, Durant exterior mirror, leather-rimmed steering wheel, basket-weave trim on lower dash, and larger deco strips on bumpers and lower body. The S also weighed less than the standard 911, tipping the scales at 2,272 pounds. Cost: U.S. $6,990.

Targa (from Italian, meaning "shield") also debuted, with zippered "soft" plastic rear window, removable roof, and roll bar "B" pillar.

Other production changes to the basic 911 included new door handles and turned aluminum trim replacing the wood on the dash.

Competition / Sport: A 911 entered in the 1965 Monte Carlo Rally (January 1965) finished fifth overall. The car was basically stock with larger rear brakes, a rear anti-roll bar, seatbelts, a rear wiper, 22-gallon fuel tank, rally instruments, Boge shocks, and special engine tuning.

The 911R was the first lightweight competition series of the 911. It weighed about 1,800 pounds using fiberglass front fenders, doors, trunk and engine lids, bumpers, and a Scheel racing seat. Plexiglas was used for the side and rear windows. Wheels were 6x15 front, 7x15 rear Fuchs alloys. Twenty-two of these cars were built in the fall of 1967.

Dimensions:	1965–1968 911
Wheelbase:	87 inches
Height:	52 inches
Width:	63.4 inches
Weight:	2,380 pounds (911R weighed 1,810 pounds)
Fuel tank capacity	16.4 gallons

0 Series – Produced until July 1967

Year	Model	Chassis Serial No.	Engine Serial No.	Produced
1964	Prototype	13 321–13 333[1]	N/A	13
1965				
(9/64–12/64)	911	300001–300235	900001–900360 (901/01)	235
(1/65–7/65)		300236–303390	900361–903550 (901/01)	3,154
1966	911	903551–907000	907001–909000 (901/05)	1,709
1967	911 Coupe	305101–308522	909001–912050 (901/06)	3,421
	911 Targa[2]	500001–500718	911191–912050 (901/05)	718
	911S Coupe	305101S–308523S	960001–962178 (901/02)	1,823[3]
	911S Targa	500001S–500718S	961141–962178 (901/02)	483

Racing Chassis

1965 Monte Carlo Rally	Chassis No. 303075-076, 303085
1967 911S Rallye	Chassis No. 306655S-657S
1967 911R	Chassis No. 307670–671, 305876, 11899001R–118990019R

Engines

Type 901/01

> September 1964 to July 1966
> 2-liter (1,991-cc) six-cylinder boxer (flat-opposed) SOHC
> 80-millimeter bore x 66-millimeter stroke
> 9.0:1 compression ratio
> Air-cooled, dry sump lubrication

---

[1] Porsche historians agree about the number of prototypes but they differ about the numbering of the chassis. Dennis Adler, in *Porsche 911 Road Cars*, says that 13 330 and 13 331 were used in developing the four-cylinder 912. Peter Morgan, in his *Original Porsche 911*, states that the chassis numbers were 13 321–13 330, 13 352, and 300001-2. Morgan says that 235 1965 models were made during 1964 as 1965 models and agrees that 1967 production began with 305101. Tobias Aichele, in *Porsche 911, Forever Young*, concurs with Morgan's prototype chassis numbers in one section of his book, but then reverts to the 13 321–13 333 sequence in his chronological listing. He claims that 13 330 and 13 331 were the 912 predecessors but also lists the latter as 13 352. Aichele says that only 232 cars were made before production stopped on December 23, 1964. Furthermore, he maintains that the first car of 1965 bore chassis number 300 235 as of January 4, 1965. The difficulty of verifying these early chassis numbers is made even more difficult because of the factory's reliance on handwritten record-keeping during this early period and the constant changes during the development and testing process.

[2] Targa production began in December 1966.

[3] The 911S models were included in the same range of serial numbers as those listed for Coupes and Targas. The "S" designation will be stamped after the serial number on an S model. The production numbers listed above were taken from an April 1991 article that appeared in The Esses, the newsletter for the Early 911S Registry. Early 911 production records contain a number of inconsistencies, so it is difficult to present an exact production count. According to Vern Lyle, author of *The Esses* article, "Mr. [Olaf] Lang in Technical Service at the Factory" confirmed the 1967 911S totals presented.

1967 was also the debut year for the Targa, which featured a removable plastic rear window.

Biral cylinders, cast alloy pistons
39-millimeter intake/35-millimeter exhaust valves
8-bearing forged crankshaft
2 Solex triple choke carburetors
Marelli distributor
130 horsepower @ 6,100 rpm
128 foot-pounds torque @ 4,200 rpm

Type 901/05 same as 901/01 except as of February 1966 Weber 40 IDA carburetors replaced the Solexes; used August 1966 to July 1967
Type 901/06

Three-into-one heat exchanger/exhaust system
Decreased valve overlap on camshafts
Bosch ignition system
130 horsepower @ 6,100 rpm
128 foot-pounds torque @ 4,200 rpm

Type 901/02

Used in the 911S
9.8:1 compression ratio
Three-into-one heat exchanger/exhaust system
Forged light alloy pistons
Soft nitrided forged steel connecting rods
42-millimeter intake/38-millimeter exhaust valves
Weber 40 IDS carburetors
160 horsepower @ 6,600 rpm
132 foot-pounds torque @ 5,200 rpm
Bosch ignition system

Racing Engines
Type 901/20

Used in the 906 race car in 1965
80-millimeter bore x 66-millimeter stroke
2.0-liter, 1,995 cc
10.3:1 compression ratio
45-millimeter intake/39-millimeter exhaust valves

Twin-plug cylinder heads
Weber 46 IDA carburetors
210 horsepower @ 8,000 rpm
152 foot-pounds torque @ 6,200 rpm
Type 901/21
    Used in 906 racing car in 1966/67
    Same as 901/20 except:
    Slide valve mechanical fuel injection
    220 horsepower @ 8,000 rpm

Transmissions

Type 901/0 five-speed to July 1965
Type 902/1 five-speed
Type 902/0 four-speed (offered in the United States only 1967 911)
Type 901/02 five-speed 911S
Optional gear ratios in 1967:
        901/51–"Nurburgring" sportier gear ratios
        901/52–hillclimb gear ratios
        901/54–"Le Mans" high-speed race circuits

Exterior Colors

1964–65	1966–67
Standard	**Standard**
6401 Slate Gray	6601 Slate Gray
6402 Ruby Red	6602 Polo Red
6403 Enamel Blue	6603 Gulf Blue
6404 Light Ivory	6604 Light Ivory
6405 Champagne Yellow	6605 Bahama Yellow
6406 Irish Green	6606 Irish Green
6407 Signal Red	6607 Sand Beige
	6608 Aga Blue
	6609 Black
Special Order	**Special Order**
6410 Dolphin Gray	30868 Burgundy Red
6411 Togo Brown	30736 Maroon
6412 Bali Blue	P2002 Tangerine
6413 Black	30847 Metallic Dark Red
	16153 Champagne Yellow
	R1007 Signal Yellow
	R1012 Canary Yellow
	17656 Lido Gold
	17657 Medium Ivory
	62109 Metallic Dark Green
	62162 Velvet Green
	62163 Leaf Green
	62164 Sea Green

Special Order

Special Order *(continued)*
62165 Golden Green
62166 Olive
R6001 Signal Green
R6016 Turkey Green
52254 Crystal Blue
R5009 Prussian Blue
R5012 Pastel Blue
R5013 Ultra Blue
52300 Metallic Blue
R8007 Sepia Brown
80342 Coffee Brown
75741 Stone Gray
75742 Light Gray
R7030 Cloudy Gray
70192 Beige Gray
95043 Black
96024 Silver Metallic

Interior
Vinyl (standard), leather (optional):
    Red, Black, Brown, or Beige
Seat inlays:
    Basket-weave leatherette in above colors
    Hounds-tooth check cloth:
        Black/Red/White, Black/White, or Black/Brown/White
Carpet was Black (more of a charcoal gray) in a square-weave pattern

Options
Per 1965 Factory List:

9101	Hubcap with painted emblem (901 361 031 00)
9107	Phoenix 165HR15 tires
9108	Dunlop SP 165HR15 tires
9118	Chrome wheels (901 361 013 22)
9127	Left-side outside mirror (901 731 111 00)
9128	Right-side outside mirror (901 731 111 00)
9131	Talbot outside mirror, left (644 731 111 00)
9132	Talbot outside mirror, right (644 731 111 00)
9189	Sisal floor mats (901 551 102 15)
9198	Velouran floor mats (901 551 101 15)
9200/9201	Lap belt, left & right (644 803 901 01)
9204/9205	Lap and diagonal belt, left & right (644 803 901 03 or 06)
9208	U.S.-approved lap belt
9217	Traveling kit
9220/9221	Bumper guards, front left (901 505 031 21), front right (901 505 032 21), and rear (901 505 033 21). Note: front bumper guards standard on U.S. cars

9224	Koni shock absorbers, front (901 341 067 05), rear (901 333 051 12)
9229	Gas heater (901 572 051 30)
9230	Supplementary electric blower
9237/9238/9239	Black leather suitcases in 3 sizes
9248	Canvas suitcase, red & black tartan pattern
9261	Canvas bag, red & black tartan pattern
9264	SKAI-Dur suitcase in black
9265	300-millimeter wood-rim steering wheel (901 347 082 01) Note: a 400-millimeter wood wheel was standard in 1965 and 1966; 911S had a leather-rim wheel as standard equipment.
9266	Horn button, black (901 347 802 001)
9267	Raised steering wheel hub, 30 millimeters closer to driver (901 347 082 11)
9290	Rear wiper
9293	Halogen H-3 bulb fog lights (644 631 912 03) Note: Hella 128 fog lamps were standard equipment for all including U.S. cars. These optional lights were not legal for the US.
9400	Special paint, non-metallic
9403	Special paint, metallic
9425	Leather interior
9427	Seats raised by 20 millimeters
9428	Leather seats only, left (901 521 001 50), right (901 521 002 50)
9442/9443	Headrest (644 521 087 05)
9444/9445	Leather headrest (644 521 085 13)
9446/9447	Leatherette headrest (644 521 085 07)
9474	Electric sunroof (901 564 003 65)
9481	Catacolor tinted glass, all windows
9482	Catacolor tinted windshield
9483	Catacolor tinted rear window
9505	Roof rack (901 801 010 00)
9506	Leather straps for roof rack (901 801 953 00)
9507	Roof-mounted ski rack (901 801 015 20)
Radios:	Blaupunkt (Bremen, Frankfurt, Frankfurt – United States, Koln, New Yorker); Becker (Monte Carlo, Europa, Mexico)

In 1967 an optional 100-liter (26.4-gallon) fuel tank was offered. The Fuchs alloy wheels (4.5x15 inches) that were standard on the 1967 911S were optional on the 911.

The 911R was standard with a white exterior. Other colors were available by special order.

Chapter Two
1968

The 911 model lineup expanded with new European models and special emission-controlled models for the United States. The 911T (Touring) was offered at a lower price and with a lower-performance (110-horsepower) engine in Europe. The base model 911 (130 horsepower) became the 911L (Lux) and included the vented disc brakes of the 911S. The 911S was offered only in Europe and had as an added feature light alloy brake calipers. The United States received the 911 and 911L models but they differed from their European counterparts. The 911L for the United States was equipped like the European 911S except for the 130-horsepower emissions-regulated (air pump) engine that it shared with the base U.S. 911. Cars destined for the United States also featured side marker lights, amber in front and red in the rear. The 911T was the only model equipped with solid brake discs.

The Sportomatic four-speed semi-automatic transmission was offered for the first time in the 1968 model year, costing an additional $280 on U.S. models.

Windshield wipers on all models were painted black and park on the left side of the windshield. All models were equipped with a dual circuit braking system.

The base U.S. 911 was $6,190; a U.S. Model 911L coupe was $6,790; and a 911L Targa, $7,190.

A Series – Produced from August 1967 to July 1968

Model	Chassis Serial No.	Engine Serial No.	Produced
911 Coupe (U. S.)	11830001–11830473	3280001–3281606 (901/14) 3380001–3380463 (901/17 Sporto)	473
911 Coupe (Karmann)	11835001–11835742	3080001–3080655 (901/06) 3180001–3180347 (901/07 Sporto)	742
911 Targa	11880001–11880268	3080001–3080655 (901/06) 3180001–3180347 (901/07 Sporto)	268
911L Coupe	11810001–11810720	3080001–3080655 (901/06) 3180001–3180347 (901/07 Sporto)	720
911L Coupe (U. S.)	11805001–118055449	3280001–3281606 (901/14) 3380001–3380464 (901/17 Sporto)	5449
911L Targa	11860001–11860307	3080001–3080655 (901/06) 3180001–3180347 (901/07 Sporto)	307
911L Targa (U. S. includes Sporto)	11855001–11865134	3280001–3281606 (901/14) 3380001–3380464 (901/17 Sporto)	5134
911T	11820001–11820928	2080001–2081754 (901/03)	928

Model	Chassis Serial No.	Engine Serial No.	Produced
911T (Karmann)	11825001–11825683	2080001–2081754 (901/03)	683
911T Targa	11870001–11870521	2080001–2081754 (901/03)	521
911S	1180001–11801267	4080001–4081549 (901/07) 4180001–4180227 (901/08 Sporto)	1267
911S Targa	11850001–11850442	4080001–4081549 (901/07) 4180001–4180227 (901/08 Sporto)	442

Porsche revised its serial number system in 1968 to an eight-digit format that included codes for the model, model year, and production version. The first two digits "11" designated a 911. The third digit was the model year, "8" for 1968. The fourth digit was the production version. In 1968, this fourth digit had the following designations:

> 0 = S Coupe
> 1 = 911 Coupe
> 3 = U. S. 911 Coupe
> 5 = S Targa
> 6 = L Targa
> 7 = T Targa
> 8 = U. S. Targa

Racing Chassis

Lightweight versions of the 911T using 911S engines, referred to as 911T/R, were used for competition. There were also lightweight racing versions of the 911L. Their chassis numbers fall within the regular production serial numbers.

The 911L (Lux) was made only in 1968 and came to the United States as a well-equipped but lower-power substitute for the 911S.

Engines

Type 901/06 continued in 911L except in the United States (designated
901/07 with Sportomatic)

Type 901/02 continued in 911S, which was not imported to the United
States (designated 901/08 with Sportomatic)

Type 901/03 fitted to 911T, which was not imported to the United States
The 901/03 is the same as the 901/06 except:
Cast-iron cylinders
8.6:1 compression ratio
Simplified 8-bearing camshaft
Altered cam timing
42-millimeter intake valves/38-millimeter exhaust valves
110 horsepower @ 5,800 rpm
116 foot-pounds torque @ 4,200 rpm
Marelli instead of Bosch ignition
Designated 901/13 with Sportomatic

Type 901/14 with emission controls fitted to U.S. 911 and 911L
The Type 901/14 is the same as the 901/06 except:
Weber 40 IDAP carburetors
Exhaust gas recalculation
130 horsepower @ 6,100 rpm
128 foot-pounds torque @ 4200 rpm
Designated 901/17 with Sportomatic transmission

*The 911R model was a limited-production run of lightweight
competition cars.*

Racing Engines

Type 901/22
Used in 911R in 1967/68. Same as 901/20 except:
210 horsepower @ 6,200 rpm
Weber 46 IDA carburetors

Type 901/23 and 901/24

Racing Engines *(continued)*

Mechanical fuel injection
210 horsepower and 180 horsepower, respectively
Type 901/30, serial nos. 3880001–3880028

911 rally engine. Same as 901/02 except:
Weber 46 IDA carburetors
39-millimeter intake/35-millimeter exhaust valves
9.8:1 compression ratio
150 horsepower

Transmissions

Different transmission numbers reflect difference in gear ratios fitted.
Type 902/01 five-speed on 911 and 911L
Type 901/10 five-speed on 911T
Type 902/0 four-speed offered in the United States
Type 901/02 five-speed on 911S
Type 905/00 Sportomatic on 911L and 911T and U.S. 911
Type 906/00 Sportomatic on U.S. 911L
Type 906/01 Sportomatic on 911S

Exterior Colors

Standard		Special Order	
6801	Slate Gray	6821	Medium Ivory
6802	Polo Red	6822	Champagne Yellow
6803	Ossi Blue	6823	Signal Yellow
6804	Light Ivory	6824	Canary Yellow
6805	Bahama Yellow	6825	Crystal Blue
6806	Irish Green	6826	Pastel Blue
6807	Sand Beige	6827	Ultra Blue
6808	Burgundy Red	6828	Golden Green
6809	Tangerine	6829	Signal Green
		6830	Leaf Green
		6831	Turquoise Green
		6832	White (Light) Gray
		6833	Cloudy Gray
		6834	Beige (Oxford) Gray
		6835	Olive
		6836	Sepia Brown
		6837	Cocoa Brown
		6838	Black
		6851	Silver Metallic
		6852	Metallic Dark Green
		6853	Metallic Blue
		6854	Metallic Dark Red

U.S. versions of 1968 911 models (and 912s as pictured here) were the only ones to be adorned with side marker lights — amber in front and red in the rear.

Interior

911T

Standard seat inlays:

Basket-weave vinyl (leatherette) in Red, Black, Brown, or Beige

Optional seat inlays:

Corduroy in Red, Black, Cognac (dark brown), or Stone Gray

Hounds-tooth check cloth in Black/Red/White, Black/White, or Black/Brown/White

Leather in Red, Black, Brown, or Beige

911L and 911S

Standard seat inlays:

Grained leatherette in Red, Black, Brown, or Beige

Optional seat inlays:

Corduroy, hounds-tooth check cloth, or leather in colors listed for 911T. Carpeting matched interior color scheme. 911T used Perlon while 911S and 911L used velour.

Options

Changes from 1965–67 list:

Fuchs alloy wheels became 5.5x15 inch

911 R decal set, including positive side stripes ("P-O-R-S-C-H-E" in bold) offered but no other parts from this model were available

Blaupunkt Boston radio available

"Luggage Deposit" offered as replacement for rear seats on Targas

Chapter Three

1969

The first major overhaul of the 911 took place with the 1969 models. To improve handling, the wheelbase was lengthened by 2.4 inches (2,268 millimeters) to measure 89.4 inches. This was done by increasing the length of the rear trailing arms to move the rear wheels back without relocating the engine. The front and rear wheel openings were flared slightly to accommodate larger wheels and tires. Heating and ventilating systems were revised, with a three-speed blower fan installed and the vent windows becoming fixed except on the Targa models. The Targas also had air vents added to the exterior of the roll bar. Fixed rear glass, an option in 1968, became standard on the Targa.

Interior changes included a smaller steering wheel with padded horn button, a day-night rearview mirror mounted on the windshield, a flip-out ashtray in the center of the dash panel's lower edge, and door panels with larger storage pockets. The heat regulator control was moved to the floor next to the gearshift. A hand throttle was also installed in that location. Emergency flashers and a glovebox light also became standard equipment.

The single 45-amp battery was replaced by twin 12-volt, 35-amp batteries mounted in each fender before the front wheels. This was to increase handling balance.

Three model lines were offered in Europe and the United States: the 911T, 911E, and 911S. The S and E both had Bosch fuel injection while the T remained carbureted. The S engine now put out 170 horsepower. It also came with an extra oil cooler mounted in the right front fender. 6Jx15 wheels and 185/70VR15 tires were standard on the E and S. The T came equipped with 5.5Jx15 standard wheels. For more comfortable cruising, both the T and E offered 5.5Jx14 wheels with 185HR14 tires.

The 911E was fitted with self-leveling hydropneumatic struts that replaced the front torsion bars. Boge and Porsche collaborated on this ill-fated experiment (it was prone to leaks and collapses), which was continued as standard equipment on the E through 1972. Over the course of time, many 911Es have been converted back to shock absorbers and torsion bars.

Capacitive discharge ignition was added to all models. Air pumps disappeared from the U.S. emission controls. Both the E and S had vented discs and alloy front calipers.

U.S. prices: 911T coupe, $5,795; E coupe, $6,995; S coupe, $7,695; add $620 for Targa.

Dimensions:	**1969–73**
Wheelbase:	89.4 inches
Height:	52 inches
Width:	63.4 inches
Weight:	2,250 pounds
Fuel tank capacity:	16.4 gallons

B Series–Produced from August 1968 to July 1969

Model	Chassis Serial No.	Engine Serial No.	Produced
911T Coupe	11900001–11900343	6190001–6192455 (901/03)	343
		6193001–6193297 (901/13 Sporto)	
		6195001–6197292 (901/16 U.S.)	
		6198001–6198184 (901/19 U.S. Sporto)	
911T Coupe (Karmann)	119120001–119123561	6190001–6192455 (901/03)	3,561
		6193001–6193297 (901/13 Sporto)	
		6195001–6197292 (901/16 U.S.)	
		6198001–6198184 (901/19 U.S. Sporto)	
911T Targa	119100001–119111282	6190001–6192455 (901/03)	282
		6193001–6192455 (901/13 Sporto)	
		6195001–6197292 (901/16 U.S.)	
		6198001–6198184 (901/19 U.S. Sporto)	
911E Coupe	119200001–119200954	6190001–6192455 (901/09)	954
		6298001–6298583 (901/11 Sporto)	
911E Coupe (Karmann)	119220001–119221014	6190001–6192455 (901/09)	1,014
		6298001–6298583 (901/11 Sporto)	
911E Targa	119210001–119210858	6290001–6292455 (901/09)	858
		6298001–6298583 (901/11 Sporto)	
911S Coupe	119300001–119301492	6390001–6392126 (901/10)	1,492
911S Targa	119310001–119310614	6390001–6392126 (901/10)	614

Porsche added another digit to its chassis serial numbers in 1969. The first two digits still designated the model ("11" for 911) and the third was still the model year ("9" for 1969).The fourth number was now the engine fitted: 1 = 911T, 2 = 911E, 3 = 911S. The fifth number was the body: 0 = Coupe, 1 = Targa, 2 = Karmann built. The last four digits were the sequential individual build numbers.

Engines
Type 901/03 fitted in 911T same as A series except for the following changes:

Magnesium crankcase
770-watt alternator
Designated 901/13 with Sportomatic

Type 901/09 fitted in 911E same as A series 911L except for the following changes:

9.1:1 compression ratio

Original 901/01 camshafts
Bosch mechanical fuel injection
770-watt alternator
Bosch CD ignition
140 horsepower @ 6,500 rpm
129 pounds-feet torque @ 4,500 rpm
Designated 901/11 with Sportomatic
Type 901/10 fitted in 911S same as A series except for the following changes:
9.9:1 compression ratio
Bosch mechanical fuel injection
45-millimeter intake valves/39-millimeter exhaust valves
Magnesium crankcase
770-watt alternator
Bosch CD ignition
Oil cooler mounted in right front fender
170 horsepower @ 6,800 rpm
134 pounds-feet torque @ 5,500 rpm
Type 901/16 fitted in the United States only 911T:
Weber 40 IDTP3C carburetors
Designated 901/19 with Sportomatic

Transmissions
Different transmission numbers reflect a difference in gear ratios fitted.
Type 901/06 fitted to 911T except the United States
Type 901/12 fitted to 911T U.S.
Type 901/07 fitted to 911E and 911S
Type 901/06 fitted to 911E U.S.
Type 901/13 fitted to 911S U.S.
Type 905/13 Sportomatic

Exterior Colors

Standard		**Special Order**	
6801	Slate Gray	R5013	Ultra Blue
6802	Polo Red	52300	Metallic Blue
6803	Ossi Blue	52254	Crystal Blue
6804	Light Ivory	R5012	Pastel Blue
6805	Bahama Yellow	62165	Lime Green
6806	Irish Green	R6001	Signal Green
6807	Sand Beige	62163	Bush Green
6808	Burgundy Red	62109	Dark Green Metallic
6809	Tangerine	R6016	Turkey Green
		75742	Gray White
		R7030	Fortuna Gray
		70192	Beige Gray
		62166	Olive

Standard

Special Order *(continued)*

R8007	Sepia Brown
80342	Coffee Brown
95043	Black
96024	Silver Metallic
17657	Medium Ivory
16153	Champagne Yellow
R1007	Signal Yellow
R1012	Canary Yellow
30847	Dark Red Metallic

Interior

Vinyl (standard), Leather (optional)
Colors: Black, Brown, or Beige
Seat inlays:
    Basket-weave, vinyl or leather:
        Black, Brown, or Tan
    Hounds-tooth check cloth:
        Black/White, or Black/Brown/White
    Corduroy:
        Black, Brown, or Tan
Carpet:
    911E and 911S:
        Black (charcoal gray) velour
    911T:
        Black or Brown Perlon

The 1969 911 had a longer wheelbase, but this S Targa still has a soft rear window, even though glass was available starting in 1968.

Options

9107	Phoenix 165VR15 tires
9108	Dunlop SP165VR15 tires
9120	Fuchs forged alloy wheels
9121	Chrome-plated wheels
9168/69	Outside thermometer
9186	Engine compartment lamp
9189/90	Velourian floor mats, Sportomatic
9198/99	Velourian floor mats, manual transmission
9216	Traveling kit, 911S
9218	Traveling kit, 911T
9219	Traveling kit, U.S. models
9222	Bumper guards
9232	Air conditioning
9239	Leather tie-down straps for rear seat
9249	Leather suitcase fitted to rear seats
9250	Leather shirtcase fitted to rear seats
9263	Luggage deposit replacement for rear seats
9268	Leather-wrapped steering wheel
9273	Quartz-iodine headlamps
9278	U.S. safety equipment
9283	Emergency flasher light
9291	Quartz-iodine fog lamps, yellow lenses
9292	Quartz-iodine fog lamps, white lenses
9297	Power radio antenna
9298	Radio interference suppressor kit
9303	Radio antenna
9307	Radio speaker
9320	Blaupunkt Bremen radio
9322	Blaupunkt Frankfurt radio
9323	Blaupunkt Frankfurt U.S. radio
9325	Blaupunkt Koln radio
9326	Blaupunkt New Yorker U.S. radio
9327	Blaupunkt Boston U.S. radio

9340	Becker Monte Carlo radio
9341	Becker Europa radio
9342	Becker Europa U.S. radio
9349	Becker Grand Prix radio
9350	Becker Grand Prix U.S. radio
9356	Tonneau for Targa
9388/89	Recaro sport seats
9400	Special paint
9403	Special paint from outside the color book and Silver Metallic
9420	Long-range driving lamps, above the bumper mount
9421	Fog lamps, above the bumper mount
9428	Leather seats with hounds-tooth check inlay
9437	Headrest, hounds-tooth check cloth
9438	Headrest, corduroy
9439	Headrest, leather
9440	Headrest, leatherette
9480	Tinted glass, Targa
9481	Tinted glass, coupe
9482	Tinted windshield only
9483	Tinted rear window, coupe only
9484	Electrically heated rear window, coupe
9485	Electrically heated, tinted glass rear window, coupe
9499	Fuel tank, 100 liters, 26 U.S. gallons (not available in the United States in 1969 or 1970)
9503	Roof luggage rack with straps for skis
9508	Roof rack for Targa
9512	Electrically heated, fixed glass, tinted rear window for Targa
9520	Stainless-steel muffler skirt
9521	Towing hook, rear
9574	Limited-slip differential
9581	Sportomatic transmission
9590	Five-speed transmission

Chapter Four

1970-1971

1970: Porsche ceased production of the 912. The 914, a Volkswagen-Porsche joint venture, took its place as an entry-level automobile. In its six-cylinder format, the 914 was equipped with the 2.0-liter engine from the 1969 911T.

The T, E, and S models continued as the mainstay of the 911 line, but now carried an engine enlarged to 2.2 liters (the cylinder bore was increased to 84 millimeters). The new engines also bene-fitted from bigger valves. A larger 225-millimeter clutch was fitted to all cars, and the 911T came with a standard four-speed transmission. The Sportomatic was dropped as an option for the S. The T did receive ventilated brake discs, making all 911s so equipped.

Externally, revised and safer door handles were added. Inside, the dashboard gauges were mounted using rubber rings, making removal for repairs/adjustments less complicated. U.S. models were fitted with a warning buzzer to indicate when the keys were left in the ignition switch. A steering lock was also added to the column. And for the first time, undercoating was applied to all models. A rear window wiper and power windows became available as options.

1971: Three-speed windshield wipers with an intermittent set-ting were fitted. Crankcase oil squirters were added to engines to improve piston cooling. U.S. models had evaporative fuel controls as part of the emissions system. The fuel pump on all models was moved from the front suspension cross-member to the rear of car.

Competition/Sport: Lightweight (1,848 pounds) 911S models were offered to customers for racing.

C and D Series – Produced from August 1969 to July 1971

C Series, Model Year 1970

Model	Chassis Serial No.	Engine Serial No.	Produced
911T	9110100001–9110102418	6100001–6103000 (911/03)	2,418
		6103001–6103230 (911/06 Sporto)	
		6103501–6104547 (911/07 U.S.)	
		6105001–6107999 (911/08 U.S. Sporto)	
911T (Karmann)	9110120001–9110124126		4,126
911T Targa	9110110001–9110112545		2,545
911E	9110200001–9110201304	6108501–6109955 (911/01)	1,304
		6108001–6108374 (911/04 Sporto)	
		6200001–6202476 (911/04 Sporto)	
		6208001–6208434 (911/04 Sporto)	

Model	Chassis Serial No.	Engine Serial No.	Produced
911E (Karmann)	9110220001–9110220667		667
911E Targa	9110210001–9110210933		933
911S	9110300001–9110301744	6300001–6302480 (911/02)	1,744
911S Targa	9110310001–9110310729		729

In 1970 Porsche went to a 10-digit serial number. The first three digits were the model number, "911." The fourth digit was the model year, "0" for 1970. The fifth digit was for the engine fitted: 1 = 911T, 2 = 911E, and 3 = 911S. The sixth digit designated body type: 0 = coupe, 1 = Targa, and 2 = Karmann built. The last four numbers were the sequential individual build numbers. This same system applied to the 1971 models (D series) depicted in the following chart.

D Series, Model Year 1971

Model	Chassis Serial No.	Engine Serial No.	Produced
911T	9111100001–9111110583	6110001–6113475 (911/03)	583
		6119001–6119190 (911/06 Sporto)	
		6114001–6118119 (911/07 U.S.)	
		6119501–6119728 (911/08 U.S. Sporto)	
911T (Karmann)	9111120001–9111121934		1,934
911T USA	9111110001–9111113476		3,476
911E	9111200001–9111201088	6210001–6211767 (911/01)	1,088
911E Targa	9111210001–9111210935	6218001–6218260 (911/04 Sporto)	935
911S	9111300001–9111301430	6310001–6311959 (911/02)	1,430
911S Targa	9111310001–9111310788		788

Racing Chassis

1970:
911S Rallye 2.2-liter
Chassis No. 9110300001-003, 9110300949-0950
911S 2.3-liter
Chassis No. 9110300001-0003
911S 2.4-liter Prototype
Chassis No. 911030949
1971:
911S Safari
Chassis No. 9111300637, 0683, 0612, 0589, 0561
The above chassis are examples of the racing version of the 911S, referred to internally as 911 S-T models. Equipment, engines, and

25

gearboxes varied depending upon whether the cars were prepared for rallying or racing. To reduce weight, interiors were stripped and thinner sheet metal, aluminum, or fiberglass components were used. Fuel tanks were enlarged to 110 liters (29.04 gallons) and space-saver spare tires fitted. Cars were ordered as a 911S with option code M470 deleted, which left out most of the standard road-going equipment.

Engines

C Series

Type 911/03 fitted to 911T. Same as B Series 911T except:

Bore increased to 84-millimeter, stroke the same at 66-millimeter

Displacement 2.2 liters, 2,195 cc

Compression ratio is 8.6:1

Zenith 40 TIN carburetor

46-millimeter intake valves/40-millimeter exhaust valves

125 horsepower @ 5,800 rpm

130 foot-pounds torque @ 4,200 rpm

Bosch CD ignition

Designated 911/06 with Sportomatic

Type 911/07 fitted to 911T United States. Same as 911/03 except for emissions tuning:

Designated 911/08 with Sportomatic

Type 911/01 fitted to 911E (including the United States). Same as B Series 911E except:

Bore 84-millimeter x stroke 66-millimeter

Displacement 2.2 liters, 2,195 cc

Valves 46-millimeter intake/40-millimeter exhaust

901/06 camshafts

155 horsepower @ 6,200 rpm

141 foot-pounds torque @ 4,500 rpm

Designated 911/04 with Sportomatic

Type 911/02 fitted to 911S (including United States). Same as B Series except:

Bore 84-millimeter x stroke 66-millimeter

Displacement 2.2 liter, 2,195 cc

Valves 46-millimeter intake/40-millimeter exhaust

180 horsepower @ 6,500 rpm

147 foot-pounds torque @ 5,200 rpm

D Series

Same as C Series

Racing Engines

Type 911/20, 1970

85-millimeter bore x 66-millimeter stroke, 2,247 cc

46-millimeter intake/40-millimeter exhaust valves

Fuel injection

10.3:1 compression ratio
230 horsepower @ 7,800 rpm
170 foot-pounds torque @ 6,200 rpm
Type 911/21, 1971–72
87.5-millimeter bore x 66-millimeter stroke, 2,380 cc
46-millimeter intake/40-millimeter exhaust valves
Fuel injection
10.3:1 compression ratio
250 horsepower @ 7,800 rpm
188 foot-pounds torque @ 6,200 rpm
Type 911/22, 1971
Same as 911/20 except for:
Weber 46 IDA carburetors
Same horsepower and torque as 911/20
Type 911/70, 1971
86.7-millimeter bore x 70.4-millimeter stroke, 2,492 cc
46-millimeter intake/40-millimeter exhaust valves
Mechanical injection
10.3:1 compression ratio
270 horsepower @ 8,000 rpm
191.6 foot-pounds torque @ 5,300 rpm

Transmissions
Clutch size increased from 215 millimeter to 225 millimeter
Type 911/00, four-speed fitted to 911T
Type 911/01, five-speed fitted to 911T, E, S
Type 905/20, Sportomatic fitted to 911T and 911E
D Series same as above

*The 1970 911T Targa carried over the longer wheelbase
introduced in 1969 but with a 2.2-liter engine.*

Exterior Colors

C Series, 1970

The factory paint code changed to four digits. The last two digits for Targas end in "10."

Standard Colors

Paint Code (Targa/Coupe)	Color Chart No.	Color
1110/1111	131	Light Ivory
1410/1414	116	Signal Orange
1510/1515	213	Irish Green
2310/2323	018	Tangerine
2610/2626	222	Conda Green
1310/1313	022	Bahia Red
1810/1818	325	Albert Blue
2010/2020	321	Pastel Blue
2410/2424	017	Burgundy
8010/8080	925	Silver Metallic
8410/8484	324	Metallic Blue
8110/8181	021	Metallic Red
8310/8383	221	Metallic Green

Special Order

Paint Code (Targa/Coupe)	Color Chart No.	Color
7910/7979	023	Light Red
7210/7272	114	Signal Yellow
2910/2929	115	Canary Yellow

The 1970 911S had 180 horsepower.

Paint Code (Targa/Coupe)	Color Chart No.	Color *(continued)*
6210/6262	117	Light Yellow
4610/4646	132	Medium Ivory
7810/7878	217	Signal Green
7710/7777	218	Leaf Green
6510/6565	22	Turquoise Green
7310/7373	320	Crystal Blue
6610/6666	326	Glacier Blue
1610/1616	327	Adriatic Blue
6410/6464	340	Turquoise
3910/3939	414	Olive
7410/7474	415	Sepia Brown
7610/7676	620	Light Gray
7510/7575	622	Beige (Oxford) Gray
1010	700	Black

D Series, 1971
Standard Colors

Paint Code (Targa/Coupe)	Color Chart No.	Color
2410/2424	017	Burgundy Red
2310/2323	018	Tangerine
1310/1313	022	Bahia Red
1410/1414	116	Signal Orange
1110/1111	131	Light Ivory
8810/8888	133	Gold Metallic
1510/1515	213	Irish Green
8310/8383	221	Metallic Green
2610/2626	222	Conda Green
2010/2020	321	Pastel Blue
8410/8484	324	Metallic Blue
1810/1818	325	Albert Blue
8610/8686	330	Gemini Blue Metallic
8010/8080	925	Silver Metallic
8110/8181	021	Metallic Red
7910/7979	023	Light Red
7210/7272	114	Signal Yellow
6210/6262	117	Light Yellow
4610/4646	132	Medium Ivory
7810/7878	217	Signal Green
7710/7777	218	Leaf Green
6510/6565	220	Green Turquoise

Special Order

Paint Code (Targa/Coupe)	Color Chart No.	Color
7310/7373	320	Crystal Blue
6610/6666	326	Glacier Blue
1610/1616	327	Adriatic Blue
6410/6464	340	Turquoise
3910/3939	414	Olive
7410/7474	415	Sepia Brown
7610/7676	620	White Gray
7510/7575	622	Beige Gray
1010	700	Black

Interior

See 1969 B Series. C and D Series were unchanged from 1969.

Options

New for 1970:

> Electric window lifts
>
> ZF limited-slip differential with either a 40 percent or 80 percent locking factor
>
> 5.5Jx15-inch Mahle cast magnesium wheels for 911T
>
> 5.5Jx14-inch Fuchs alloy (standard on 911E) for 911T

New for 1971:

> Heated windshield
>
> H3-bulb fog and driving lights for the United States
>
> 100-liter (26-U.S. gallon) fuel tank dropped from list

Chapter Five

1972–1973

1972: T, E, and S models carried over with several significant changes. Engine size increased to 2.4 liters by increasing the stroke to 70.4 millimeters. Compression ratios were also decreased to allow engines to run on regular fuel, primarily because of the U.S. requirement for unleaded gas. Forged crankshafts were used in all engines, including the T. The U.S. T joined the E and S by using mechanical fuel injection while other countries still had Weber-equipped T models. At 140 horsepower, the U.S. T had a 10 horsepower advantage over the carburetted versions. The E now made 165 horsepower and the S, 190 horsepower.

The dry-sump oil tank was relocated from a position behind the right rear wheel to a spot ahead of it. An external filler door was added so that oil could be added into the tank from outside the car. This move was made to improve the handling balance of the car.

Hydropneumatic front struts became optional on all models including the E, which reverted to the MacPherson design of the T and S. The rear suspension mounting points were altered slightly and the swing arms revised, actually increasing the wheelbase by 3 millimeters. Boge shocks were standard on the E and T with Konis still mounted on the S. Konis and Bilsteins were options on the E and T. The S had 15-millimeter anti-roll bars front and rear while anti-roll bars were options for the T and E models.

The increased torque of the larger engine necessitated a stronger transmission. The new Type 915 used a conventional H pattern with fifth gear up and to the right.

The standard wheels and tires on the T were 5.5Jx15, nonchromed, steel units with Dunlop 165/70HR15 tires. The E in many markets came with 6Jx15 steel wheels shod with Dunlop 185/70VR15 tires. The S had 6Jx15 Fuchs forged alloys with Michelin 185/70VR tires that were also optional on the T and E. The S came with a steel front spoiler that was available as an option on other models. A 911T could be fitted with all the S options except the motor.

A rectangular driver's-side external rearview mirror replaced the round Durant mirror. Other external changes included a black-colored grille on the engine lid. U.S. cars were fitted with inertia reel seatbelts and seatbelt warning buzzers.

1973: Unwary service station attendants pumping fuel into the external oil filler opening of 1972 911s forced Porsche to put the oil tank back in its old location. The tank was now made of stainless steel.

ATS cast alloy "cookie cutter" wheels (6Jx15) were introduced as standard equipment on the E. The auxiliary oil cooler in the right front fender of the S became a labyrinth or tube-type unit.

Front air intakes changed from chrome to black plastic. Trim around the front indicator lights and taillights changed from chrome plastic to black plastic.

Side-impact door beams were added to U.S. models. Large rubber bumper guards were also fitted front and rear to U.S. cars.

In January 1973, the "1973 1/2" U.S.-spec 911Ts were fitted with Bosch K-Jetronic (CIS) fuel injection and rated at 140 horsepower.

1973 base prices (1972 prices) in U.S. dollars: 911T coupe, $7,960 ($7,250); 911E coupe, $8,960 ($7,995); 911S coupe, $10,060 ($9,495). Targa, add $800 ($735).

Competition/Sport: Porsche introduced the Carrera RS as a limited production option in both a competition and road-use version. Weight was reduced to as little as 2,117 pounds in the racing version. A 2.7-liter, 210-horsepower engine (that was actually a 2.4-liter S engine with the bore increased to 90 millimeters) powered the Carrera. To strengthen the cylinders, Nikasil, nickel-silicon carbide coating, was applied to the surface, a technique carried over from the 917 race cars. Flared rear wheel arches and a duck tail rear spoiler distinguished the cars along with optional "Carrera" script side decals the same color as the spokes of the 6Jx15 front, and 7Jx15 rear, alloy wheels. The racing versions are called RSRs.

E and F Series – Produced from August 1971 to July 1973
E Series, Model Year 1972

Model	Chassis Serial No.	Engine Serial No.	Produced
911T	9112500001–9112501963	6520001–6523284 (911/57)	1,963
911T Targa	9112510001–9112511523	6529001–6529224 (911/67 Sporto)	1,523
911T U.S.	9112100001–9112102931	6120001–6124478 (911/51)	2,931
911T U.S. Targa	9112110001–9112111821	6129001–6129293 (911/61 U.S. Sporto)	1,821
911E	9112200001–9112201124	6220001–6221765 (911/52)	1,124
911E Targa	9112210001–9112210861	6229001–6229248 (911/62 Sporto)	861
911S	9112300001–9112301750	6320001–6322586 (911/53)	1,750
911S Targa	9112310001–9112310989	6329001–6329147 (911/63 Sporto)	989

Ten-digit serial numbers were used for the 1972 model year. The first three digits again stood for the model, "911," and the fourth was the year, "2." The fifth digit was the engine code as follows: 1 = 911T, 2 = 911E, 3 = 911S, 5 = 911T with carburetors. The sixth digit was the body style: 0 = coupe and 1 = Targa. As in the prior year, the last four digits were the sequential individual build numbers.

F Series, Model Year 1973

Model	Chassis Serial No.	Engine Serial No.	Produced
911T	9113500001–9113501875	6530001–6533239 (911/59)	1,875
911T Targa	9113510001–9113511541	6539001–6539197 (911/67 Sporto)	1,541
911T U.S.	9113100001–9113101252	6130001–6131926 (911/51)	1,252
911T Targa U.S.	9113110001–9113110781	6139001–6139149 (911/61 Sporto)	781
911T US, CIS[1]	9113101501–9113103444	6133001–6136092 (911/91)	1,944
911T Targa U.S., CIS	9113110001–9113112302	6139301–6139502 (911/96 Sporto)	1,302
911E	9113200001–9113201366	6230001–6232125 (911/52)	1,366
911E Targa	9113210001–9113211055	6239001–6239319 (911/62 Sporto)	1,055
911S	9113300001–9113301430	6330001–6332231 (911/53)	1,430
911S Targa	9113310001–9113310925	6339001–6339136 (911/63 Sporto)	925
911 RS Carrera	9113600001–9113601590	6630001–6631551 (911/83)	1,590

[1] U.S. 911T switched from mechanical to K-Jetronic (CIS) fuel injection in January 1973.

The 10-digit serial number for 1973 was essentially the same as for 1972 except that the fourth digit (model year) was a "3," and the fifth digit engine code was as follows: 1 = 911T, 2 = 911E, 3 = 911S, 5 = 911T with carburetors, and 6 = 911 Carrera.

The 1972 911S (2.4 liter, 190 horsepower) was the first to come with a steel front spoiler and the last year for chrome air intakes. The steel spoiler was an option on the Model E and T, as well.

The ducktail spoiler was a hallmark of the 1973 Carrera RS models. The fiberglass rear deck with an aluminum frame was actually an option on models outside Germany where government safety officials determined the hard edges of the tail were not "pedestrian friendly."

Racing Chassis
1972
911S 2.5
Chassis No. 9112300041, 0047
1973
Carrera 2.7 Safari
Chassis No. 9113600288, 0285
Carrera 2.8 RSR
Total of 55 cars within the range of Chassis No. 9113600386-1549

Included are customer cars: 0386, 0557, 0601, 0614, 0636, 0643, 0659, 0701, 0705, 0714, 0727, 0755, 0756, 0760, 0782, 0784, 0785, 0791, 0817, 0837, 0847, 0853, 0865, 0871, 0885, 0894, 0915, 0921, 0940, 0960, 0991, 0997, 1008, 1033, 1045, 1054, 1088, 1099, 1113, 1134, 1155, 1159, 1183, 1196, 1329, and 1497, 1523.

Prototypes were: 9113600019 R1, 9113600020 R2, 9113600307 R3, 9113600328 R4, 9113600576 R5, 9113600588 R6, 9113600686 R7, and 9113600974 R8

Engines

E Series

Type 911/57 fitted to 911T except for U.S. versions. Same as C and D Series except for:

    Same 84-millimeter bore x increased stroke to 70.4 millimeter

    Called 2.4-liter despite 2,341 cc

    Fully counterweighted crankshaft

    Oil jets for piston cooling

    Camshafts same as 911/51

    Zenith 40 TIN carburetors

    7.5:1 compression ratio

    130 horsepower @ 5,600 rpm

    144 foot-pounds torque @ 4,000 rpm

    Designated 911/67 with Sportomatic

Type 911/51 fitted to 911T United States

    84-millimeter bore x 70.4-millimeter stroke

    2.4-liter, 2,341 cc

    Mechanical fuel injection

    7.5:1 compression ratio

    140 horsepower @ 5,600 rpm

    148 foot-pounds torque @ 4,000 rpm

    Designated 911/61 with Sportomatic

Type 911/52 fitted to 911E

    84-millimeter bore x 70.4-millimeter stroke

    2.4-liter, 2,341 cc

    Mechanical fuel injection

    8.0:1 compression ratio

    165 horsepower @ 6,200 rpm

    151 foot-pounds torque @ 4,500 rpm

    Designated 911/62 with Sportomatic

Type 911/53 fitted to 911S

    84-millimeter bore x 70.4-millimeter stroke

    2.4-liter, 2,341 cc

    Mechanical fuel injection

    8.5:1 compression ratio

    190 horsepower @ 6,500 rpm

    158 foot-pounds torque @ 4,000 rpm

    Designated 911/63 with Sportomatic

F Series

Same as E Series except for :

Type 911/91 fitted to 911T United States beginning January 1973

    Bosch K-Jetronic (CIS) replaced mechanical injection of 911/51

    8.0:1 compression ratio

    140 horsepower @ 5,700 rpm

148.5 foot-pounds torque @ 4,000 rpm

Designated 911/96 with Sportomatic

Type 911/83 fitted to Carrera RS

Bore increased to 90-millimeter x 70.4-millimeter stroke

2.7-liter, 2,681 cc

Nikasil cylinders

Mechanical fuel injection

8.5:1 compression ratio

210 horsepower @ 6,300 rpm

188.4 foot-pounds torque @ 5,100 rpm

Racing Engines

Type 911/72, 1972 911 RSR

92-millimeter bore x 70.4-millimeter stroke, 2,808 cc

Mechanical fuel injection

49-millimeter intake/41.5-millimeter exhaust valves

10.3:1 compression ratio

308 horsepower @ 8,000 rpm

217 foot-pounds torque @ 6,200 rpm

Type 911/73, 1972

89-millimeter bore x 66-millimeter stroke, 2,462 cc

Mechanical fuel injection

10.3:1 compression ratio

275 horsepower @ 8,000 rpm

Transmissions

1972

New transmission named 915, moved first gear into the H pattern, was stronger and had a better lubrication system than 901

Type 915/12 four-speed standard in most markets

Type 915/02 five-speed version

Type 925/21 four-speed Sportomatic for European 911T and 911E

Type 925/00 four-speed Sportomatic for the United States and RoW 911T and 911E

Type 925/01 four-speed Sportomatic for 911S

1973

Same as 1972 except for :

Type 915/08 five-speed developed for Carrera RS

Exterior Colors

Standard Colors, 1972

Color Code	Color Name
018	Tangerine
022	Bahia Red
025	Aubergine
114	Signal Yellow
117	Light Yellow

Color Code	Color Name *(continued)*
131	Light Ivory
225	Emerald Green
325	Albert Blue
415	Sepia Brown

Special Order, 1972

Color Code	Color Name
019	Gulf Orange
024	Rose Red
116	Signal Orange
132	Ivory
213	Irish Green
218	Leaf Green
226	Lime Green
227	Jade Green
326	Glacier Blue
328	Gulf Blue
329	Oxford Blue
341	Royal Purple
414	Olive
622	Beige Gray
700	Black
133	Gold Metallic
224	Metallic Green
324	Metallic Blue
330	Gemini Metallic
925	Silver Metallic

Standard Colors, 1973

Color Code	Color Name
022	Bahia Red
225	Emerald (Viper) Green
415	Sepia Brown
131	Light Ivory
025	Aubergine
117	Light Yellow
018	Tangerine
114	Signal Yellow

Special Order, 1973

Color Code	Color Name
019	Gulf Orange
024	Rose Red
116	Signal Orange
132	Ivory
213	Irish Green
218	Leaf Green
226	Lime Green

Color Code	Color Name *(continued)*
227	Jade Green
326	Glacier Blue
328	Gulf Blue
329	Oxford Blue
341	Royal Purple
414	Olive
622	Beige Gray
700	Black
144	Gold Metallic
230	Metallic Green
334	Metallic Blue
335	Gemini Metallic
936	Silver Metallic

Interior

1972 and 1973
Leatherette (vinyl) standard:
    Black, Brown, Tan, Red, or Blue
Leather optional:
    Black, Brown, or Tan
Seat inlays:
    Perforated, leather or vinyl:
        Black, Brown, or Tan
    Hounds-tooth check cloth:
        Black/White, or Brown/White/Black
    Corduroy:
        Black, Brown, or Tan
    Plaid cloth (Madras):
        Orange, Blue, or Tan
Carpet:
    Perlon for 911T and 911E
    Velour for 911S and Carrera RS:
        Black, Charcoal, or Brown

Options

Porsche began listing options with the "M" prefix in 1970
Significant changes or additions from the prior year:
M471   *Carrera RS Sport*: Lightweight version of the 911S intended
    for club racers. Weight: 2,150 pounds. Thinner steel used in
    fenders, doors, roof, trunk lid, and other parts of the body.
    Fiberglass bumpers. Thinner window glass. Sound insulation
    deleted. Rubber mats instead of carpeting. Door pockets and

The U.S. version of the 1973 911 came with large rubber bumper extensions on the front and rear. The car pictured also is equipped with optional driving lights that were mounted through the front grilles.

Options *(continued)*

armrests deleted. Rear seats, clock, and passenger sun visor removed. Recaro sport seats fitted. Single battery. Duck tail rear spoiler. Wheels: 6x15 front, 7x15 rear. Tires: Pirelli Cinturato CN36 or Dunlop SPD4; 195/60VR15 front, 215/60VR15 rear. Two hundred Sport versions were made. Cost: about $10,200 (United States)

M472   *Carrera RS Touring*: De Luxe version of Carrera RS with carpeting, soundproofing, opening rear windows, steel rear bumper, rear seats; equipped very similar to the 911S. A total of 1,308 Touring versions made. Cost: $11,000 (United States)

M492   *2.8-liter Carrera RS*R: Extended fender flares, roll bar, 917 brakes, and 2.8-liter engine. Fifty-five versions were made. There were also 17 RSH (Homologation) lightweight FIA approved for racing specials made of the Carrera RS. Cost: about $24,000 (United States)

M425   Rear wiper

M650   Electric sunroof

M409   Sport seats

Chapter Six

1974–1977

1974: U.S. safety laws had a big impact on the appearance of the 911 for the 1974 model year. The protruding new bumpers were made of aluminum with rubber side bellows that were designed to absorb the impact of a 5-mile-per-hour collision. A small front spoiler was part of the revised front bodywork that required moving the indicator lights into the bumper. The lower side sills were extended to cover the jacking post holes and a red plastic strip bearing the word "Porsche" was added below the engine lid filling the space between the taillights.

The T and E model designations were dropped from the model line. The base model was now simply called 911 while the S became more comparable to the E of previous years. The Carrera went from being a limited-production special to assume the previous S role as the top-of-the-line performance model. All models had a larger 2.7-liter engine. The RoW Carrera continued with the 210-horsepower, mechanical fuel injection version that debuted in 1973, but the U.S. Carrera, to meet emissions standards, had the same 175-horsepower K-Jetronic version as the 911S. The base 911's 2.7-liter was fitted with the K-Jetronic fuel injection and developed 150 horsepower.

A Targa was added to the Carrera lineup in 1974. The duck-tail spoiler of the 1973 Carrera RS was an option on the Carrera except in Germany. The U.S. 911 and 911S had four-speed manual transmissions as standard equipment but most were delivered with the five-speed option.

The new front end design resulted in the 911 reverting to a single 66-amp battery. An optional 88-amp battery was available as well. A larger fuel tank increased capacity to 21.1 gallons and a space-saver spare tire also became standard equipment, with U.S. cars getting an electric air compressor to pump it up. RoW cars came with a container of compressed air.

A nonfolding fiberglass Targa top replaced the folding version as standard equipment. The latter remained as a necessary option for cars fitted with air conditioning, which took up top storage space in the trunk.

Suspension changes included a simpler, front anti-roll bar design and forged aluminum trailing arms (7.7 pounds lighter than the previous year) at the rear. The anti-roll bar was mounted under the body. The 911 and 911S models were equipped with 16-millimeter front anti-roll bars while the Carrera came with a 20-millimeter front bar. Additionally, the Carrera had an 18-millimeter rear anti-roll bar. Both of these larger bars were options (as a set) on the 911 and 911S. The Carrera also came equipped with Bilstein sport shocks.

The 1974 911 was the first to have safety bumpers with rubber bellows extensions and a 2.7-liter engine.

The most visible changes to the interior were new high-backed seats with integrated headrests. The armrest storage compartments had top-mounted flaps for easier access. Side window defogger vents were added at each end of the dash. The Carrera had a three-spoke, leather-wrapped steering wheel.

The standard wheels for U.S. 911s remained steel 5.5Jx15 with 165/70HR15 tires while RoW cars got the ATS cookie cutters. The 911S came with 6Jx15 ATS wheels and 185/70VR15 tires. For the Carrera, 6Jx15 Fuchs alloys and 185/70VR tires were mounted in front, 7Jx15 wheels with 215/60VR tires in the rear.

Prices (United States): Base 911, $9,950; 911S, $11,875; and Carrera, $13,575. $850 was added for Targa versions. Popular option costs were five-speed manual transmission, $250; air conditioning, $1,125; power sunroof, $615; and alloy wheels, $605. The cost for a Sportomatic transmission was $425.

Competition/Sport: A series of Carrera RS 3.0 and Carrera RSR 3.0 models were produced. The most famous variations of these cars were the International Race of Champions (IROC) cars delivered to Roger Penske and Mark Donohue for use in the initial race series.

1975: The base 911 was eliminated from the U.S. model lineup. For the American customers, Porsche divided production of the 911S and Carrera into 49-state and California versions based on emissions controls. The 49-state cars were fitted with an air pump, whereas the California cars also were fitted with thermal reactors and exhaust gas recirculation (EGR) systems. A new and quieter exhaust equipped all 911 models.

The whale-tail spoiler replaced the duck tail on the Carrera and a new front spoiler was added. Carrera models also had body-color headlight surrounds and external mirrors. The Carrera Targa roll bar was finished in matte black.

ATS (commonly known as "cookie cutter") wheels replaced the steel wheels as standard for the base 911. Carrera wheels were upgraded to 7Jx15 in front and 8Jx15 in rear. The suspensions of U.S. cars were raised to meet headlight height regulations.

Turbo model production began in February 1975. Initial models were fitted with 7Jx15 front, and 8Jx15 rear Fuchs alloys with black centers. Tire sizes were 185/70VR and 215/60VR, respectively. Though Dunlop tires were standard, the new Pirelli P7 soon became a popular option.

A Silver Anniversary 911 option (M426) was offered on 911 and 911S coupes and Targas. In all, 1,063 Silver Anniversary cars were produced: 154 RoW coupes, 150 RoW Targas, 510 U.S. coupes, and 249 U.S. Targas.

1976: The hand throttle was eliminated after equipping a vacuum-controlled warm-up regulator on the K-Jetronic fuel injection. The Sportomatic option went from a four-speed to a three-speed. The folding Targa top again became standard equipment. The 911S was the only U.S. model besides the Turbo. For the first time, Porsche offered a six-year warranty against rust, because the bodies were built of galvanized steel.

In the engine bay, a 5-blade engine cooling fan replaced the 11-blade unit on all cars, except on the Turbos.

Options included headlight washers, "Tempostat" cruise control, and thermostatic cockpit temperature control.

Outside mirrors were painted the same as the body color and were electronically controlled. All cars were fitted with electronic speedometers. The 911S was fitted with A-type cast-iron front brake calipers that had the same pad size as the alloy S calipers.

On Turbos, Pirelli P7 tires, 205/55VR15 front, and 225/50VR15 rear, became standard equipment. Optional were 16-inch wheels. The Turbo cost $25,850 in the United States. A 911S was priced at $13,845 and the Targa version at $14,795.

1977: United States, Canadian, and Japanese models were fitted with air injection pumps, thermal reactors, and EGR to meet those countries' stricter emissions laws.

The 915 transmission was improved to make engagement of first gear easier and other shifts smoother. Cars fitted with the Sportomatic—the Carrera 3.0, Turbos, and all U.S. cars—received power brake boosters.

The 911's rear suspension received two-piece trailing arms to make adjusting the ride height easier. The M470 Comfort option included power windows, softer Bilstein shocks and 185HR14 tires for a smoother ride, and a fuel-cutoff-switch speed governor that kept top speed under the tires' 130-mile-per-hour speed rating.

Two central fresh air vents were added to the dash, improving the effectiveness of the optional air conditioning. An optional center console (required with air conditioning and standard on the Turbo and Carrera) accommodated air-conditioning controls, radio controls, a microphone, and cassette storage. To combat auto theft, the Targa models no longer had operating vent wings. Another anti-theft measure for all models was the rotary door-lock release combined with shorter door-lock buttons that disappeared when locked.

On Turbos, a boost gauge was fitted for the first time, and 7Jx16 front, and 8Jx16 rear, wheels became standard. Tires were 205/55VR16 and 225/50VR16. Anti-roll bar sizes were 20 millimeters in front and 18 millimeters at the back. The price of a U.S. Turbo was $28,000.

Competition / Sport: The development of the production Turbo was a major step toward Porsche moving from the normally aspirated Carrera RSR to the Turbo RSR 934 and 935 race cars that were built for new FIA regulations beginning in 1976. Group 4 were special GT models while Group 5 allowed more extensive modifications.

Dimensions	1974–77
Wheelbase:	89.4 inches
Height:	52.8 inches
Width:	65 inches
Weight, 911:	2,370–2,470 pounds
Weight, Turbo:	2,630 pounds
Fuel tank capacity:	21.0 gallons

The 1975 Carrera featured a "whale tail" rear spoiler. The whale tail first appeared on the Carrera RSR and was carried over to the Turbo. Rubber edges were considered more "pedestrian friendly" than the ducktail.

G Series – Produced from August 1973 to July 1974

Model	Chassis Serial No.	Engine Serial No.	Produced
911	9114100001–9114104014	6140001–6146625 (911/92)	4,014
911 Targa	9114110001–9114113110	6149001–6149517 (911/97 Sporto)	3,110
911S	9114300001–9114301359	6340001–6342804 (911/93)	1,359
911S Targa	9114310001–9114310898	6349001–6349236 (911/98 Sporto)	898
Carrera	911460001–9114601036	6640001–6641456 (911/83)	1,036
Carrera Targa	911461001–9114610433		433
Carrera U.S.	9114400001–9114400528	6340001–6342804 (911/93)	528
Carrera Targa U.S.	9114410001–9114410246		246

Racing Chassis

Carrera RS, RSR 3.0	9114609001–9114609109	6640001–6640200 (911/77)	109

Note: In addition to the above, 15 cars were produced as IROC cars sold to Roger Penske. Their chassis serial nos. are: 9114600016, 0025, 0035, 0037, 0040, 0042, 0050, 0059, 0075, 0085, 0090, 0100, 0111, 0116, 0124.

While the Porsche factory lists serial numbers between 9114609001 and 9114609109, it is not clear if a car was produced for each number in that range.

The 10-digit serial number included "4" as the fourth digit for model year. The code for the fifth digit, engine, was as follows: 1 = 911, 3 = 911S, 4 = Carrera United States, 6 = Carrera.

Engines

Type 911/92 fitted to 911
> 90-millimeter bore x 70.4-millimeter stroke
> 2.7-liter, 2,687 cc
> 8.0:1 compression ratio
> K-Jetronic fuel injection
> 150 horsepower @ 5,700 rpm
> 175 foot-pounds torque @ 3,800 rpm
> Designated 911/97 with Sportomatic

Type 911/93 fitted to 911S
> 90-millimeter bore x 70.4-millimeter stroke
> 2.7-liter, 2,687 cc
> 8.5:1 compression ratio
> K-Jetronic fuel injection
> Alusil replaced Nikasil cylinders
> 175 horsepower @ 5,800 rpm
> 167 foot-pounds torque @ 4,000 rpm

Designated 911/98 with Sportomatic
Type 911/83 fitted to Carrera
Same as prior year

Racing Engines

Type 911/74, 1974 3.0 RSR and IROC
95-millimeter bore x 70.4-millimeter stroke, 2,994 cc
Mechanical fuel injection
49-millimeter intake/41.5-millimeter exhaust valves
10.3:1 compression ratio
315 horsepower @ 8,000 rpm
231 foot-pounds torque @ 6,500 rpm
Type 911/75, 3.0 RSR
95-millimeter bore x 70.4-millimeter stroke
3.0-liter, 2,994 cc
Slide valve mechanical fuel injection
10.1 compression ratio
310 horsepower @ 8,000 rpm
231 foot-pounds torque @ 6,500 rpm
Type 911/76, RSR Turbo
83-millimeter bore x 66-millimeter stroke
2.1-liters, 2,143 cc
47-millimeter intake/40.5-millimeter exhaust valves
Turbocharger
6.5:1 compression ratio
480 horsepower @ 8,000 rpm
340 foot-pounds torque @ 5,900 rpm

Transmissions

Type 915/06 five-speed manual fitted to 911 and 911 Carrera
Type 915/16 standard four-speed manual on U.S. cars
Type 915/40 five-speed manual fitted to 911S
Type 925/02 four-speed Sportomatic

Exterior
Standard Colors

Color Code	Color Name
027	Guards Red
042	Peru Red
116	Signal Orange
117	Light Yellow
137	Lime Green
156	Orange
336	Mexico Blue
408	Bitter Chocolate
516	Sahara Beige
908	Grand Prix White

Special Order

Color Code	Color Name
009	Magenta
024	Rose Red
025	Aubergine
036	Salmon Metallic
213	Irish Green
227	Jade Green
249	Emerald Green Metallic
250	Ice Green Metallic
253	Birch Green
328	Gulf Blue
334	Metallic Blue
335	Gemini Metallic
341	Royal Purple
354	Bahama Blue
406	Gazelle Metallic
414	Olive
432	Copper Brown Metallic
631	Steel Blue Metallic
700	Black
936	Silver Metallic

Interior

Leatherette (vinyl) standard:
> Light grain pattern (000.551.615.11):
>> Dark Red, Tan, or Black
>
> Basket-weave (999.551.002.41):
>> Dark Red, Tan, or Black
>
> Roy Flex heavy grain (999.551.001.40):
>> Red, Blue, or Black

Leather (999.551.071.41), optional:
> Red, Tan, Black

Madras (plaid) (999.551.031.40):
> Red, Blue, Brown

Additional no-cost options:
> Shetland seat centers (999.551.032.41):
>> Dark Red, Tan, or Black
>
> Tweed seat centers (999.551.034.40):
>> Red/White, Black/White/Turquoise, or Tan
>
> Twill seat trim (999.551.035.40):
>> Dark Red, Tan, or Black

Carpets:
> Nylon velour (999.551.052.40):
>> Red, Blue/Green, or Tan
>
> Perlon (999.551.051.41):
>> Red, Tan, or Black

Special velour (999.551.061.41):
Red, Tan, or Black

Options

M060	Auxiliary heater
M093	Manual right-side mirror
M102	Rear window defroster
M197	88-amp battery
M220	Limited-slip differential (80 percent)
M261	Power right-side mirror
M288	High-pressure headlight washers
M402	Koni shock absorbers
M404	18-millimeter rear anti-roll bar
M405	Protective lacquer finish, orange
M406	Protective lacquer finish, green
M407/8	Front seats raised 26 millimeter
M409	Recaro sport seats
M410	Recaro sport seat, driver only
M412	Front oil cooler
M414	Oil pressure/level gauges, basic 911 only
M416	Leather steering wheel w/raised hub
M417	Porsche script on doors, orange
M419	Porsche script on doors, green
M422	Blaupunkt Bamberg stereo
M425	Rear window wiper
M427	Carrera script on doors, gold
M428	Protective lacquer finish, gold

Options

M429	Rectangular, under-bumper fog light, white lens
M430	Rectangular, under-bumper fog light, yellow lens
M432	Protective lacquer finish, black
M436	Folding Targa top
M438	Porsche script on doors, gold
M439	Porsche script on doors, black
M440	Manual antenna (left side) w/speakers and wiring
M441	Power antenna (right side) w/speakers and wiring
M443	Tinted side/front windows; heated windshield and rear window
M446	Chrome trim, Carrera
M449	Blaupunkt Lubeck stereo
M450	Alloy wheels, black, Carrera only, front: 6Jx15 w/185/70VR15 tires, rear: 7Jx15 w/215/60VR15 tires
M451	Same as 450, comet diamant metallic
M452	Blaupunkt Frankfurt radio
M454	Blaupunkt Coburg radio
M458	Alloy wheels, 6Jx15 w/185/70VR15 tires, silver green diamant metallic

M459	Same as 458, comet diamant metallic
M460	Same as 458, gray blue metallic
M461	Power antenna w/wiring
M462	Carrera script on doors, black
M468	Air compressor
M469	Black headliner
M474	Bilstein shocks
M477	Alloy wheels, 6Jx15 w/185/70VR15 tires, included w/911S
M477	Alloy wheels, Carrera only, front: 6Jx15 w/185/70VR15 tires, rear: 7Jx15 w/215/60VR15 tires
M481	Five-speed transmission
M482	Engine compartment light
M485	Alloy wheels, 5.5Jx15 w/165/HR15 tires
M490	Manual radio antenna w/wiring
M497	Self-starter
M498	Delete model designation from engine lid
M559	Air conditioning
M560	Electric sunroof
M561	Power windows
M562	Intermittent wipers
M565	Sport steering wheel
M567	Tinted windshield
M568	Tinted side and windshield
M569	Package, M429 fog light and M571 rear fog light
M571	Rear fog light

H Series – Produced from August 1974 to July 1975

Model	Chassis Serial No.	Engine Serial No.	Produced
911	9115100001–9115101238	6150001–6152007 (911/41)	1,238
911 Targa	9115110001–9115110998	6159001–6159252 (911/46 Sporto)	998
911S	9115300001–9115300385	6350001–6350567 (911/42)	385
911S Targa	9115310001–9115310266	6359001–6359105 (911/47 Sporto)	266
911S U.S. 49 state[1]	9115200001–9115202310	6450001–6452440 (911/43)	2,310
911S Targa U.S.	9115210001–9115211517	6459001–6459135 (911/48 Sporto)	1,517
Carrera	9115600001–9115600518	6650021–6650712 (911/83)	518
Carrera Targa	9115610001–9115610197		197
Carrera U.S.	9115400001–9115400395	6450001–6452440 (911/43)	395
Carrera Targa U.S.	9115410001–9115410174	6459001–6459135 (911/48 Sporto)	174
Turbo	9305700001–9305700284	6750001–6750297 (930/50)	284

[1] Includes all cars with California emissions.

The 10-digit serial number designated the following: The first three digits were the model, 911 or 930 (Turbo). The fourth digit was the year, 5 = 1975. The fifth digit identified engines as follows: 1 = 911, 2 = 911S United States, 3 = 911S, 4 = Carrera United States, 6 = Carrera, 7 = Turbo. The sixth digit was body style: 0 = Coupe, 1 = Targa. The remaining four digits were the individual build numbers in sequential order.

Engines

Type 911/41 fitted to RoW 911
> 90-millimeter bore x 70.4-millimeter stroke
> 2.7-liter, 2,687 cc
> 8.0:1 compression ratio
> K-Jetronic fuel injection
> 150 horsepower @ 5,700 rpm
> 175 foot-pounds torque @ 3,800 rpm
> Designated 911/46 with Sportomatic

Type 911/42 fitted to RoW 911S
> 90-millimeter bore x 70.4-millimeter stroke
> 2.7-liter, 2,687 cc
> 8.5:1 compression ratio
> K-Jetronic fuel injection
> 175 horsepower @ 5,800rpm
> 167 foot-pounds torque @ 4,000 rpm
> Designated 911/47 with Sportomatic

Type 911/83 fitted to Carrera
> Same as prior year

Type 911/43 fitted to 49-state U.S. 911S and Carrera. Same as 911/42 except:
> Air pump emissions control
> 165 horsepower @ 5,800 rpm

The 1976 Turbo Carrera (260 horsepower) was the first model of what has become an automotive legend.

167 foot-pounds torque @ 4,000 rpm

Designated 911/48 with Sportomatic

Type 911/44 fitted to California 911S and Carrera. Same as 911/42 except:

Air pump, thermal reactors, and EGR emissions control

160 horsepower @ 5,800 rpm

162 foot-pounds torque @ 4,000 rpm

Designated 911/49 with Sportomatic

Type 930/50 fitted to Turbo

95-millimeter bore x 70.4-millimeter stroke

3.0-liter, 2,994 cc

Single KKK Turbocharger

K-Jetronic fuel injection

Nikasil barrels, forged alloy pistons, and aluminum case

6.5:1 compression ratio

260 horsepower @ 5,500 rpm

253 foot-pounds torque @ 4,000 rpm

Transmissions

Type 915/48 four-speed manual fitted to RoW 911

Type 915/43 five-speed manual fitted to RoW 911

Type 915/45 four-speed manual fitted to RoW and U.S. 911S

Type 915/40 five-speed manual fitted to RoW 911S, U.S. 911S, and U.S. Carrera

Type 915/16 four-speed manual fitted to RoW Carrera

Type 915/06 five-speed manual fitted to RoW Carrera

Type 925/04 four-speed Sportomatic for all models

Type 930/30 four-speed fitted to Turbo

Exterior
Standard Colors

Color Code	Color Name
027	Guards Red
042	Peru Red
117	Light Yellow
137	Lime Green
156	Orange
336	Mexico Blue
408	Bitter Chocolate
516	Sahara Beige
908	Grand Prix White

Special Order

Color Code	Color Name
009	Magenta
024	Rose Red
025	Aubergine
036	Salmon Metallic

A 1977 Targa with ATS "cookie cutter" wheels.

Color Code	Color Name *(continued)*
116	Signal Orange
213	Irish Green
227	Jade Green
249	Emerald Green Metallic
250	Ice Green Metallic
253	Birch Green
328	Gulf Blue
334	Metallic Blue
335	Gemini Metallic
341	Royal Purple
354	Bahama Blue
406	Gazelle Metallic
414	Olive
432	Copper Brown Metallic
631	Steel Blue Metallic
700	Black
936	Silver Metallic

Interior
Leatherette (vinyl) standard:
  Smooth (no grain) (000.551.615.03):
    Black, Tan, or Ivory
  Light grain pattern (999.551.001.41):
    Dark Red, Tan, or Black
  Basket-weave (light pattern) (999.551.002.41):
    Dark Red, Tan, or Black
  Basket-weave (heavy pattern) (000.551.615.12):
    Ivory, Tan, or Black
  Roy Flex light grain (999.551.021.41):
    Red, Blue, or Brown

Interior *(continued)*
Leather (999.551.071.41), optional:
　　Red, Tan, or Black
Madras (plaid) (999.551.031.40):
　　Red, Blue, or Brown
Additional no-cost options:
　　Shetland seat centers (999.551.032.41):
　　　　Dark Red, Tan, or Black
　　Tweed seat centers (999.551.034.40):
　　　　Red/White, Black/White/Turquoise, or Tan
　　Twill seat trim (999.551.035.40):
　　　　Dark Red, Tan, or Black
Turbo options:
　　Tartan Dress (999.551.081.40):
　　　　MacLaughlan Red, Black Watch Green, or Dress
　　　　　Mackenzie Brown/Beige
Carpets:
　　Nylon velour (999.551.052.40):
　　　　Red, Tan, or Black
　　Perlon (999.551.051.41):
　　　　Red, Tan, or Black
　　Special Velour (999.551.061.41):
　　　　Red, Tan, or Black
　　Velour pile (Carrera only) (999.551.075.41):
　　　　Yellow, Dark Green, Burgundy, Tan, or Dark Blue/Gray
　　Also available on Jubilee car:
　　　　Dark Red or Orange

Options
Significant changes or additions from 1974:
M426　Silver Anniversary Model. Special silver metallic paint,
　　"25 Jahre" dash plaque, and the following options as part of
　　the package:
　　M102　　Two-stage heated rear window
　　M288　　Headlamp washers
　　M422　　Blaupunkt Bamberg radio
　　M461　　Power radio antenna
　　M458　　6Jx15 silver metallic finish alloy wheels
　　M404　　18-millimeter rear anti-roll bar
　　M496　　Black trim
　　M565　　380-millimeter sport steering wheel
　　M481　　Five-speed gearbox

Production total: 1,063 cars worldwide—154 RoW Coupes, 150 RoW
Targas, 510 U.S. Coupes, and 249 U.S. Targas

J Series – Produced from August 1975 to July 1976

Model	Chassis Serial No.	Engine Serial No.	Produced
911	9116300001–9116301868	6360001–6363029 (911/81)	1,868
911 Coupe, Japan	9116100001–9116100130	6160001–6160140 (911/41)	130
911 Targa	9116310001–9116311576		1,576
911 Sportomatic		6369001–6369435 (911/86 Sporto)	
911S U.S. 49-state	9116610001–9116610479	6460001–6462305 (911/82)	2,079
911S Targa US	9116210001–9116212175[2]	6656001–6561837 (911/84 CA)	2,175
911S US w/Sportomatic		6569001–6569160 (911/89 Sporto)	
Carrera 3.0	9116600001–9116601093	6660001–6661385 (930/02)	1,093
Carrera 3.0 Targa	9116200001–9116202079		
Carrera 3.0 w/Sportomatic		6669001–6669212 (930/12 Sporto)	479
Turbo	9306700001–9306700644	6760001–6760157 (930/50) 6760301–6760808 (930/52)	644
Turbo US	9306800001–9306800530	6860001–6860541 (930/51)	530

[2] Includes all 911S models with California emissions.

The 10-digit serial numbers designated the following: The first three digits were the model, 911 or 930 (Turbo). The fourth digit was the year, 6 = 1976. The fifth digit identified engines as follows: 2 = 911S United States , 3 = 911, 6 = Carrera, 7 = Turbo, 8 = Turbo United States. The sixth digit was body style, 0 = Coupe, 1 = Targa. The remaining four digits were the individual build numbers in sequential order.

Racing Chassis
934 Turbo:
    Chassis No. 9306700151–9306700180, 9306700540.

Engines
Type 911/81 fitted to RoW 911
    90-millimeter bore x 70.4-millimeter stroke
    2.7-liter, 2,687 cc
    8.5:1 compression ratio
    K-Jetronic fuel injection
    165 horsepower @ 5,800 rpm

Engines *(continued)*

    176 foot-pounds torque @ 4,000 rpm

    Designated 911/86 with Sportomatic

Type 911/82 fitted to 49-state United States 911S

    90-millimeter bore x 70.4-millimeter stroke

    2.7-liter, 2,687 cc

    8.5:1 compression ratio

    K-Jetronic fuel injection

    Air pump emissions control

    165 horsepower @ 5,800rpm

    176 foot-pounds torque @ 4,000 rpm

    Designated 911/89 with Sportomatic

Type 911/84 fitted to California 911S. Same as 911/82 except:

    Air pump, thermal reactors, and EGR emissions control

    160 horsepower @ 5,800 rpm

    162 foot-pounds torque @ 4,000rpm

    Designated 911/89 with Sportomatic

Type 930/02 fitted to Carrera 3.0

    95-millimeter bore x 70.4-millimeter stroke

    3.0-liter, 2,994 cc

    8.5:1 compression ratio

    K-Jetronic fuel injection

    200 horsepower @ 6,000 rpm

    188 foot-pounds torque @ 4,200 rpm

    Designated 930/12 with Sportomatic

Type 930/50 fitted to Turbo

    Same as prior year

Type930/51 fitted to U.S., Canada, and Japan Turbos. Same as 930/50 plus:

    Emissions controls (air pump and thermal reactors)

    245 horsepower @ 5,500 rpm

    253 foot-pounds torque @ 4,000 rpm

Racing Engines

Type 930/71 fitted to 934 race car

    3.0-liter, 2,994 cc

    Turbocharger with 1.35 bar boost

    6.5:1 compression ratio

    530 horsepower @ 7,000 rpm

    434 foot-pounds torque @ 5,400 rpm

Type 930/72 fitted to factory 935 Turbo

    92.8-millimeter bore x 70.4-millimeter stroke

    2.8-liter, 2,856 cc

    6.5:1 compression ratio

    590 horsepower @ 7,900 rpm

    438 foot-pounds torque @ 5,400 rpm

Transmissions

Type 915/49 four-speed manual fitted to RoW 911

Type 915/44 five-speed manual fitted to RoW 911 and U.S. 911S

Type 915/16 five-speed manual fitted to RoW and U.S. Carrera

Type 925/04 three-speed Sportomatic for all models

Type 930/30 four-speed fitted to Turbo

Type 930/32 four-speed fitted to Turbo with 50-series tires

Exterior
Standard Colors

Color Code	Color Name
027	Guards Red
107	Continental Orange
117	Light Yellow
258	Ascot Green
305	Arrow Blue
408	Bitter Chocolate
700	Black
908	Grand Prix White

Special Order

Color Code	Color Name
009	Magenta
042	Peru Red
137	Lime Green
213	Irish Green
260	Apple Green
264	Emerald Green Metallic
265	Oak Green Metallic
266	Ice Green Metallic
304	Minerva Blue
360	Ice Blue
436	Sienna Metallic
443	Copper Brown Metallic
516	Sahara Beige
936	Silver Metallic
944	Platinum Metallic

The 1973 RSR prototype was fitted with a 2.8-liter engine and raced at Le Mans.

Interior

Leatherette (vinyl) standard:

    Smooth (no grain) (000.551.615.03):

        Black, Tan, or Ivory

    Light grain pattern (999.551.001.41):

        Dark Red, Tan, or Black

    Basket-weave (light pattern) (999.551.002.41):

        Dark Red, Tan, or Black

    Basket-weave (heavy pattern) (000.551.615.12):

        Ivory, Tan, or Black

    Roy Flex light grain (999.551.021.41):

        Red, Blue, or Brown

Leather (999.551.073.40), optional:

    Orange, Brown, Green, Blue, Dark Brown, Tan, Black, Mid
        Brown, Red, or White

Additional no-cost options:

Shetland seat centers (999.551.032.41):

    Dark Red, Tan, or Black

Tweed seat centers (999.551.034.40):

    Red/White, Black/White/Turquoise, or Tan

Twill seat trim (999.551.035.40):

    Dark Red, Tan, or Black

Tartan Dress (999.551.083.40) (All 911 models):

    MacLaughlan Red, Black Watch Green, or Dress Mackenzie
        Brown/Beige

Carpets:

    Special velour (999.551.061.41):

        Red, Tan, or Black

    Velour pile (999.551.075.41):

        Yellow, Dark Green, Burgundy, Tan, or Dark Blue/Gray

In 1974 the International Race of Champions (IROC) featured 911 RSRs.

Options

Changes or additions from prior year:

M009	Three-speed Sportomatic (no-cost option)
M220	Limited-slip differential, 80 percent or 40 percent
M392	Scottish tweed interior trim
M393/4	Rear fender decals for Turbo model
M395	Pirelli P7 205/50VR15 front, and 225/50VR15 rear tires
M399	Air conditioning
M400	Forged alloy wheels; 7Jx15 front, 8Jx15 rear w/185/70VR15 and 215/60VR15 tires (Carrera only)
M403	Aluminum trim strip lower sill
M418	Aluminum trim strip on wheel arches
M424	Automatic heating control
M454	Tempostat cruise control
M494	Dual stereo speakers on rear shelf
M496	Blacked out trim and body color–matched headlight surrounds

K Series – Produced from August 1976 to July 1977

Model	Chassis Serial No.	Engine Serial No.	Produced
911	9117300001–9117302449	6370001–6373531 (911/81)	2,449
911 Targa	9117310001–9117311724	6379001–6379322 (911/86 Sporto)	1,724
911S US	9117200001–9117203388	6270001–6276041 (911/85)	3,388
911S Targa US	9117210001–9117212747	6170001–6170273 (911/94 Japan) 6279001–6279113 (911/90 Sporto US) 6179001–6179110 (911/99 Japan Sporto)	2,747
Carrera 3.0	9117600001–9117601473	6670001–6671932 (930/02)	1,473
Carrera 3.0 Targa	9117610001–9117600646		
Carrera 3.0 w/Sportomatic		6679001–6679215 (930/12 Sporto)	646
Turbo	9307700001–9307700695	6770001–6770642 (930/52)	695
Turbo US	9307800001–9307800727	6870001-6870737 (930/53)	727

The 10-digit serial numbers designated the following: The first three digits were the model, 911 or 930 (Turbo). The fourth digit was the year, 7 = 1977. The fifth digit indicated engine as follows: 2 = 911S U.S. , 3 = 911, 6 = Carrera, 7 = Turbo, 8 = Turbo United States. The sixth digit was body style: 0 = Coupe, 1 = Targa. The remaining four digits were the individual build numbers in sequential order.

Racing Chassis

934 Turbo US   Chassis No. 9307700951–9307700960
935 Turbo   Chassis No. 9307700901–9307700913

Engines

Type 911/81 fitted to RoW 911
    90-millimeter bore x 70.4-millimeter stroke
    2.7-liter, 2,687 cc
    8.5:1 compression ratio
    K-Jetronic fuel injection
    165 horsepower @ 5,800 rpm
    176 foot-pounds torque @ 4,000 rpm
Type 911/85 fitted to all U.S. 911s (50 states)
    Air pump, thermal reactors, and EGR emissions control
    165 horsepower @ 5,800 rpm
    176 foot-pounds torque @ 4,000rpm
Type 930/02 fitted to Carrera 3.0
    95-millimeter bore x 70.4-millimeter stroke
    3.0-liter, 2,994 cc
    8.5:1 compression ratio
    K-Jetronic fuel injection
    200 horsepower @ 6,000 rpm
    188 foot-pounds torque @ 4,200 rpm
Type 930/52 fitted to RoW Turbo
    Same as 930/50
Type 930/53 fitted to U.S. Turbo
Type 930/54 fitted to Japan Turbo
    Same as 930/51 (emissions control equipped)

Racing Engines

Type 930/72 fitted to custumer 935 Turbo
    95-millimeter bore x 70.4-millimeter stroke
    3.0-liter, 2,994 cc
    6.5:1 compression ratio
    630 horsepower @ 8,000 rpm, 1.45 bar boost
    438 foot-pounds torque @ 5,400 rpm
Type 930/73 fitted to 934/935 Turbo
    3.0-liter, 2,994 cc
    Mechanical fuel injection
    6.5:1 compression ratio
    590 horsepower @ 7,500 rpm, 1.45 bar boost
    438 foot-pounds torque @ 5,400 rpm
Type 930/76 fitted to 935 Turbo
    3.0-liter, 2,994 cc
    6.5:1 compression ratio
    630 horsepower @ 7,900 rpm, 1.45 bar boost
    438 foot-pounds torque @ 5,400 rpm

Racing Engines *(continued)*

Type 930/77 fitted to 935 Turbo
>   2.8-liter, 2,875 cc
>   6.5:1 compression ratio
>   590 horsepower @ 7,900 rpm, 1.4 bar boost
>   438 ft- lbs torque @ 5,400 rpm

Transmissions

Type 915/65 four-speed manual fitted to RoW 911
Type 915/60 five-speed manual fitted to RoW 911
Type 915/61 five-speed manual fitted to U.S. 911S and
>   RoW Carrera
Type 925/16 three-speed Sportomatic for RoW models
Type 925/17 three-speed Sportomatic for U.S. models
Type 930/33 four-speed fitted to Turbo

Exterior
Standard Colors

Color Code	Color Name
027	Guards Red
106	Talbot Yellow
107	Continental Orange
117	Light Yellow
258	Ascot Green
305	Arrow Blue
408	Bitter Chocolate
700	Black
908	Grand Prix White

Special Order

Color Code	Color Name
009	Magenta
042	Peru Red
137	Lime Green
213	Irish Green
260	Apple Green
264	Emerald Green Metallic
265	Oak Green Metallic
266	Ice Green Metallic
304	Minerva Blue
360	Ice Blue
436	Sienna Metallic
443	Copper Brown Metallic
516	Sahara Beige
936	Silver Metallic
944	Platinum Metallic

The evolution of the RSR concept ultimately led to the turbo-powered 935s.

Interior

Leatherette (vinyl) standard:
  Heavy grain pattern (999.551.012.40):
    Red, Tan, or Black
  Basket-weave (light pattern) (999.551.009.40):
    Black, Lobster, or Cork
Leather (999.551.073.40), optional:
  Gold/Yellow, Dark Green, Light Green, Blue, Dark Brown, Cork, Black, Lobster, Light Red, or White
Additional no-cost options:
  Pin-stripe velour (999.551.039.40):
    Black w/White stripes, Lobster w/Black stripes, or Cork w/Black stripes
  Tartan Dress (999.551.083.40):
    MacLaughlan Red, Black Watch Green, or Dress Mackenzie Brown/Beige
Note: All of the above interiors were available on Turbo models.
Carpets:
  Velour pile (999.551.092.40):
    Yellow, Green, Dark Brown, Cork, Black, Lobster, or Light Red

Options

Significant changes or additions from the prior year:
M042   Martini racing stripes (blue/red) for Grand Prix White cars (installed on approximately 200 Turbos)
M590   Comfort Kit: 185HR14 tires on 14-inch Fuchs alloys, speed governed to 130 miles per hour, softer shock absorbers. U.S. versions also included power windows and cruise control. Sportomatic-equipped cars got power brakes. Center console.

Chapter Seven

1978–1983, 911SC

1978: The new 911SC (S for Super, C for Carrera) combined the previous year's 911S and Carrera models into one basic 911, with coupe and Targa variations, that had the 3.0-liter engine, wider rear fender flares and wheels, and other features first seen in the previous Carrera. The rear quarter windows became fixed on all models.

Standard equipment were 6Jx15 front and 7Jx15 rear wheels with 185/70VR15 front tires and 215/60VR15 rear tires. Optional were 16-inch wheels (6J front, 7J rear) with 205/55VR and 225/50VR tires, front to rear. The previous Carrera's anti-roll bars, 20-millimeter front/18-millimeter rear, also became standard on the SC. All 911SC models worldwide came equipped with power brakes.

Porsche fitted air injection pumps to all SC 3.0-liter engines, which had six variations to meet the regulations of various countries. All developed 180 horsepower. U.S. models came with catalytic converters enabling them to run unleaded gas. The 11-blade cooling fan returned. Contact points disappeared from the ignition system. A rubber-centered clutch disc also debuted. The Sportomatic became a special order option.

The Turbo engine was bored and stroked to 3.3 liters and fitted with an intercooler. A new rear wing was designed to accommodate the intercooler. The Turbo also got a 917-style brake system featuring cross-drilled vented discs and four-piston alloy calipers.

The 911SC U.S. price was $19,500; Targa, $20,775. The Turbo price was $36,700.

1979: No major changes from the 1978 SC and Turbo models. The previous year's Sportomatic was offered. Option prices were: power windows, $300; alloy wheels, $1,230; cruise control, $270; power sunroof, $795; sport seats, $330; leather seats, $680; full leather interior, $1,450; front & rear spoilers, $650; and AM/FM stereo w/cassette, $500.

1980: U.S. models became "50-state" cars, receiving oxygen sensors (Lambda sonde) and three-way catalytic converters to battle emissions. All models were equipped with reinforced, heavier lower valve covers.

In the United States, air conditioning, power windows, black window trim, and a leather-covered, 380-millimeter, three-spoke steering wheel became standard equipment. U.S. cars were also outfitted with 85-mile-per-hour speedometers.

The Turbo received a dual outlet exhaust and new tube-style oil cooler but was dropped from the U.S., Canada, and Japan model lineup.

A Sportomatic transmission was no longer offered. An optional alarm system became available for the first time from the factory.

The Weissach limited-edition 911SC model was offered in the

United States, featuring special exterior and interior colors, larger wheels, and spoilers.

The base 911SC coupe cost $27,700; the Targa, $29,150.

1981: 911SC models reverted back to steel-spring clutches after problems with rubber-centered units. Porsche improved the K-Jetronic fuel injection with a cold-start injector spray to prevent air box damage due to backfires. The factory also upgraded the braided fuel lines to seamless, stainless-steel lines. An engine compartment light was added as standard equipment. The Turbo was available again in Canada.

The first slant-nose Turbo, 932BX000619, rolled out on July 16, 1981, from the restoration shop at Zuffenhausen. This special-order conversion (*Sonderwunschen*) became an official option (M506) for the 1987 model year.

1982: An alternator with an internal voltage regulator and 1,050-watt output was added to all models. The Turbo (tea tray) rear spoiler became an option for the SC. Standard alloy wheels on the SC came with black-painted center sections. The "Ferry Porsche" limited edition model was offered for sale.

Option codes, by "M" number, were listed on the vehicle ID plate.

1983: U.S. ride heights came back in line with the rest of the world. Starting in 1975, to comply with federal 5-mile-per-hour bumper laws, U.S.-bound cars had been raised on their suspensions 9–15 millimeters in front, and 21–25 millimeters in the rear. All models were equipped with 160-mile-per-hour speedometers. A Cabriolet model debuted with a manual top and zippered, plastic rear window. Leather seats and dual heated, electrically operated external rearview mirrors were also standard on the Cabriolet. A heated glass rear window was optional for the Cabriolet.

The Turbo (still not available in the United States and Japan) received a new exhaust system.

The U.S. 911SC Cabriolet base price was $34,450. A 911SC Targa was $31,450, and the coupe sold for $29,950.

Dimensions	**1978–83**
Wheelbase:	89.4 inches
Height:	52.8 inches
Width:	65 inches
Weight, 911:	2,560 pounds
Weight, Turbo:	2,870 pounds
Fuel tank capacity	21.0 gallons

L Series – Produced from August 1977 to July 1978

Model	Chassis Serial No.	Engine Serial No.	Produced
911SC	9118300001–9118302438	6380001–on (930/03)	2,438
911SC Targa	9118310001–9118311729		1,729

Model	Chassis Serial No.	Engine Serial No.	Produced
911SC U.S. 49-state	9118200001–9118202436	6280001–on (930/04)	2436
911SC U.S. Calif.		6580001–on (930/06)	
911SC Targa U.S. 49-state	9118210001–9118212579	6280001—on (930/04)	2,579
911SC Targa Calif.	9118200001–8118212579	6580001–on (930/06)	
911SC Japan	9118309501–9118309804	6180001–on (930/05)	304
Turbo RoW	9308700001–9308700735	6780001–on (930/60)	735
Turbo Japan	9308709501–9308709561	6782001–on (930/62)	61
Turbo U.S. 49-state	9308800001–9308800461	6880001–on (930/61)	
Turbo Calif.		6881001–on (930/63)	461

The 10-digit serial numbers designated the following: The first three digits were the model, 911 or 930 (Turbo). The fourth digit was the year, 8 = 1978. The fifth digit indicated engine, 2 = 911SC United States, 3 = 911SC (RoW), 7 = Turbo (RoW), 8 = Turbo United States. The sixth digit was body style: 0 = Coupe, 1 = Targa. The remaining four digits were the individual build numbers in sequential order. (RoW) = Rest of World.

Engines

Type 930/03 fitted to RoW 911SC
> 95-millimeter bore x 704-millimeter stroke
> 3.0-liter, 2,994 cc
> 49-millimeter intake/41.5-millimeter exhaust valves
> Diecast aluminum crankcase
> Nikasil cylinders
> 11-blade cooling fan
> K-Jetronic fuel injection
> 8.5:1 compression ratio
> 180 horsepower @ 5,500 rpm
> 175 foot-pounds torque @ 4,200 rpm
> Designated 930/13 with Sportomatic

Type 930/04 fitted to 49-state U.S. and Canadian 911SC. Same as 930/03 except for:
> Catalytic converters

Type 930/05 fitted to Japan 911SC. Same as 930/04 except for:
> Catalytic converters and EGR emissions plus heat shield
> Designated 930/15 with Sportomatic

Type 930/06 fitted to California 911SC. Same as 930/04 except for:
Catalytic converters and EGR emissions
Type 930/60 fitted to RoW Turbo
95-millimeter bore x 74.4-millimeter stroke
3.3-liter, 3,299 cc
Air-to-air Intercooler
7.0:1 compression ratio
300 horsepower @ 5,500 rpm
304 foot-pounds torque @ 4,000 rpm
Type 930/61 fitted to 49-state and Canadian Turbo. Same as
930/60 except:
Thermal reactors and EGR emissions
Unleaded fuel required (96 RON)
265 horsepower @ 5,500 rpm
291 foot-pounds torque @ 4,000 rpm
Type 930/62 fitted to Japan Turbo. Same as 930/61 except:
Thermal reactors and EGR emissions plus heat shield
Type 930/63 fitted to California Turbo. Same as 930/61 except:
Thermal reactors and EGR emissions plus vacuum control
ignition retard

Racing Engines
Type 930/78 3.0 935 Turbo
3.0-liter, 2,994 cc
6.5:1 compression ratio
720 horsepower @ 7,800 rpm, 1.4 bar boost
Type 935/71 3.2 935 Turbo
95.7-millimeter bore x 74.4-millimeter stroke
3.2-liter, 3,211 cc
7.0:1 compression ratio
750 horsepower @ 8,200 rpm, 1.4 bar boost

Transmissions
Type 915/44 five-speed manual for RoW 911SC
Type 915/61 five-speed manual for all U.S. and Canadian 911SC
Type 915/15 five-speed manual for Japan 911SC
Type 930/34 four-speed manual for all Turbos

Exterior
Standard Colors

Color Code	Color Name
027	Guards Red
106	Talbot Yellow
107	Continental Orange
260	Apple Green
265	Oak Green Metallic
273	Fern Green

Color Code	Color Name *(continued)*
274	Olive Green
275	Light Green Metallic
304	Minerva Blue Metallic
305	Arrow Blue
376	Petrol Blue Metallic
408	Bitter Chocolate
443	Copper Brown Metallic
451	Mocha Brown
502	Cashmere Beige
700	Black
908	Grand Prix White
936	Silver Metallic

Interior
Leatherette (vinyl) standard:
> Heavy grain pattern (999.551.012.40):
>> Lobster, Cork, or Black
> Basket-weave (light pattern) (999.551.009.40):
>> Black, Lobster, or Cork

Leather (999.551.073.40), optional:
> Yellow, Light Green, Blue, Cork, Black, Lobster, Light Red, or White

Additional no-cost options:
> Pin-stripe velour (999.551.039.40):
>> Black w/White stripes, Lobster w/Black stripes, or Cork w/Black stripes
> Tartan Dress (999.551.083.40):
>> MacLaughlan Red, Black Watch Green, or Dress Mackenzie Brown/Beige

Note: All of the above interiors were available on Turbo models.
Carpets:
> Velour pile (999.551.092.40):
>> Yellow, Cork, Black, Lobster, or Light Red

Options
Following is a list of options that covers model years from the 1978 911SC to the 1993 Carrera 2/4. Information is not available from the Porsche factory to break out options by specific year. For this same reason, there may be minor options that are missing from the list. Beginning in 1982, M numbers were part of the Vehicle Identification Label (VIL), but in countries where an option may have been part of the standard equipment or an option package, it may not appear separately on the VIL.

1978–1993:

M09	Three-speed Sportomatic (discontinued after 1979)
M18	Sport steering wheel w/elevated hub

The 1980 SC became a "50-state" car in the U.S. at the same time when, the Turbo model (in the background) was dropped from the U.S. line.

1978–1993: *(continued)*

M20	Speedometer with dual scales (kph/mph)
M26	Activated charcoal canister
M30	Sport suspension Carrera 2 (1992–93)
M68	Bumpers w/impact absorbers
M70	Tonneau for Cabriolet
M97-99	Anniversary model, 1989
M103	Shock absorber strut adjustment
M126	Digital radio, 1982
M139	Driver's-seat heater
M148	Modified engine, 930/66
M152	Engine sound reduction kit
M154	Emissions controls
M155	Motronic for cars w/catalytic converters
M156	Reduced sound muffler
M157	Oxygen sensor and catalyst
M158	Radio: Monterey (1986) or Reno (1987)
M160	Radio, Charleston
M167	Bridgestone tires
M176	Oil cooler w/fan
M185	Retractable two-point rear seatbelts
M186	Nonretractable rear seatbelts
M187	Asymmetric headlamps
M190	Side door beams
M195	Prewired for cell phone
M197	88–amp/hr battery
M218	Front and rear license plate brackets
M220	Locking differential (40 percent)
M240	Modified for countries with poor fuel quality
M261	Passenger-side external mirror w/flat glass

M286	High-intensity windshield washer
M288	Headlight washer
M298	Prepared to run on unleaded fuel
M326	Blaupunkt Berlin radio
M327	Blaupunkt Koln radio
M328	Blaupunkt Bremen or Symphony radio
M329/330	Blaupunkt Toronto radio
M335	Retractable three-point rear seatbelts
M340	Heated passenger seat
M341	Central locking
M351	Porsche CR stereo/cassette Type DE, manual antenna, speakers
M375	Asbestos-free clutch lining
M377/8	Combination seat (left & right)
M378-380	Series seat, power vertical adjustment (left & right)
M383/387	Sports seats, power vertical adjustment (left & right)
M389	Porsche CR stereo United States radio/cassette, manual antenna, speakers
M391	Stone guard decal rear fenders
M395	Forged alloy wheels: 6Jx15 w/205 tires front, 7Jx15 w/225 tires rear
M399	Air conditioning w/o front condenser
M403	35-Year Anniversary Model, 1982
M406	Front wheel housing protection (1983–86)
M409	Sport seats, leather (left & right)
M410	Sport seats, leatherette/cloth (left & right)
M419	Rear luggage compartment replacing back seats
M424	Automatic heater control
M425	Rear wiper
M437/438	Comfort seats (left & right)
M439	Power-operated Cabriolet top
M440	Radio kit, manual antenna, door-mounted speaker, static suppressors
M441	Radio kit, power antenna, door-mounted speakers, static suppressors
M443	Tinted front and side glass; heated windshield
M444	Cabriolet
M446	Targa build kit
M451	Radio preparation, sport group
M454	Cruise control
M461	Power antenna
M462	Sekuriflex laminated windshield
M463	Clear windshield
M464	Delete air compressor and tire pressure gauge
M467	External driver-side mirror, convex glass
M468	Graduated tint windshield, green tint side glass
M469	Black headliner

M470	Delete spoilers
M473	With spoilers
M474	Sport shock absorbers
M475	Asbestos-free brake pads
M482	Engine compartment light
M483	Right-hand drive
M487	Fog lights wired through parking lights
M490	Hi-Fi sound system
M491	"Turbo Look" body
M492	H4 headlights for left-hand traffic
M494	Dual speakers on rear shelf
M496	Blacked out trim, color-coded headlight rims
M498	Delete rear model designation
M503	Speedster variant of Cabriolet
M505	Slant-nose for the United States
M506	Slant-nose, RoW
M513	Lumbar support for passenger seat
M525	Alarm w/continuous warning sound
M526	Cloth door panels
M528	Passenger-side external mirror, convex glass
M533	Alarm system
M559	Air conditioning
M565	Safety steering wheel, 380-mm diameter, leather
M566	Rectangular front fog lights
M567	Graduated tint windshield
M568	Tinted windshield and side glass
M573	Air conditioning
M577	Heated and tinted windshield
M586	Lumbar support, driver's seat
M590	Center console
M591	Bosch-Teves ABS
M592	Brake fluid warning system
M593	Bosch ABS
M594	Wabco ABS
M602	Third brake light, mounted at top of rear window
M605	Vertical headlight adjustment
M630	Police equipment
M637	Club Sport model
M650	Electric sunroof
M651	Power windows
M652	Intermittent wipers
M656	Manual steering
M659	Front fog lights (1979)
M659	On-board computer
M666	Delete lacquer and chrome preservative coating
M673	Prepared for lead-sealed odometer

M684	One-piece rear seat
M686	Blaupunkt Ludwigsburg radio
M688	Blaupunkt Boston radio
M690	CD player CD10 with radio
M691	CD player with radio: CD01, 1988; CD02, 1989–on
M701	Slant-nose
M702	930/66 engine
M930-35/945/7/8	Seat covers
M970	Floor mats
M974	Velour carpeting in luggage compartment
M980	Ruffled leather seat covering
M981	All leather trim
M986	Partial leather trim

M Series – Produced from August 1978 to July 1979

Model	Chassis Serial No.	Engine Serial No.	Produced
911SC	9119300001–9119303319	6390001–on (930/03)	3,319
911SC Targa	9119310001–9119311874		1,874
911SC U.S. 49-state	9119200001–9119202013	6290001–on (930/04)	2,013
911SC U.S. Calif.		6590001–on (930/06)	
911SC Targa U.S. 49-state	9119210001–9119211965	6290001–on (930/04)	1965
911SC Targa Calif.		6590001–on (930/06)	
911SC Japan	9119309501–9119309873	6190001–on (930/05)	373
Turbo RoW	9309700001–9309700820	6790001–on (930/60)	820
Turbo Japan	9309809501–9309809532	6791001–on (930/62)	32
Turbo U.S. 49-state	9309800001–9309801200	6890001–on (930/61)	1,200
Turbo U.S. Calif.		6891001–on (930/63)	

The 10-digit serial number designated the following: The first three digits were the model, 911 or 930 (Turbo). The fourth digit was the year, 9 = 1979. The fifth digit designated the engine as follows: 2 = 911SC U.S., 3 = 911SC (RoW), 7 = Turbo (RoW), 8 = Turbo United States. The sixth digit was body style: 0 = Coupe, 1 = Targa. The remaining four digits were the individual build numbers in sequential order.

Engines
Same as 1978

Racing Engines
Same as 1978 plus:
Type 930/79 3.12 935 IMSA
    97-millimeter bore x 70.4-millimeter stroke
    3.12-liters, 3,121 cc
    6.5:1 compression ratio
    715 horsepower @ 7,800 rpm, 1.4 bar boost

Transmissions
Type 915/62 five-speed manual for RoW 911SC
Type 915/63 five-speed manual for United States, Canada, and Japan
Type 930/34 four-speed manual for all Turbos

Exterior
Standard Colors

Color Code	Color Name
027	Guards Red
106	Talbot Yellow
265	Oak Green Metallic
274	Olive Green
275	Light Green Metallic
301	Light Blue Metallic
304	Minerva Blue Metallic
305	Arrow Blue
376	Petrol Blue Metallic
408	Bitter Chocolate
443	Copper Brown Metallic
451	Mocha Brown
463	Casablanca Beige Metallic
464	Tobacco Metallic
502	Cashmere Beige
601	Lilac
700	Black
708	Black Metallic
908	Grand Prix White
936	Silver Metallic

Interior
Leatherette (vinyl) standard:
    Heavy grain pattern (999.551.012.40):
        Brown, Cork, or Black
    Basket-weave (light pattern) (999.551.009.40):
        Black, Brown, or Cork
Leather (999.551.073.40), optional:
    Yellow, Dark Green, Blue, Cork, Black, Brown, Light Red, or White

Additional no-cost options:

Pin-stripe velour (999.551.039.40):

Black w/White stripes, Lobster w/Black stripes, or Cork
w/Black stripes

Note: All of the above interiors were available on Turbo models except leatherette. Turbo also continues the Tartan Dress Plaid option.

Carpets:

Velour cut-pile (999.551.098.40):

Yellow, Cork, Black, Brown, Dark Green, or Light Red

Options See note and listing for 1978 model year

A Program–Produced from August 1979 to July 1980

Model	Chassis Serial No.	Engine Serial No.	Produced
911SC	91AO130001–91AO134831	6300001–on (930/09)	4,831
911SC Japan		6308001–on (930/08)	
911SC U.S.	91AO140001–91AO144272	6300001–on (930/07)	4,272
Turbo	93A0070001–93A0070840	6700001–on (930/60)	840
Turbo Japan		6708001–on (930/65)	

Prior to changing over to an international standard (17-digit) chassis serial number in 1981, Porsche adopted an interim solution in the 1980 model year that still used 10 digits. The code was as follows: The first two digits were the model: 91 = 911, 93 = 930 (Turbo). The third digit was the year, A = 1980. The fourth digit indicated the plant of manufacture. The fifth digit also indicated the model, 1 = 911 and 0 = Turbo. The sixth digit was for the engine version, 3 = RoW, 4 = United States, 7 = Turbo. The remaining four digits were the individual build numbers in sequential order.

Engines

Type 930/09 fitted to RoW 911SC

Compression ratio 8.6:1

188 horsepower @ 5,500 rpm

188 foot-pounds torque @ 4,200 rpm

Type 930/07 for the United States and Canada

50-state legal

Compression ratio 9.3:1

Oxygen sensor (Lambda sonde) fitted

Three-way catalytic converter

180 horsepower @ 5,500 rpm

175 foot-pounds torque @ 4,200 rpm

Type 930/08 for Japan

Similar to 930/07

Type 930/60 fitted to RoW Turbo
> Same as 1979 except:
> Dual outlet exhaust

Type 930/65 for Japan Turbo
> Same as 1979 Type 930/64 for U.S. 49-state

No U.S. Turbo models in 1980

Racing Engines

Type 930/80 3.2 935 Turbo
> 95-millimeter bore x 74.4-millimeter stroke
> 3.3-liter, 3,164 cc
> 7.2:1 compression ratio
> 740 horsepower @ 7,800 rpm, 1.4 bar boost

Transmissions

Same as previous year

Exterior
Standard Colors

Color Code	Color Name
027	Guards Red
106	Talbot Yellow
265	Oak Green Metallic
274	Olive Green
275	Light Green Metallic
301	Light Blue Metallic
304	Minerva Blue Metallic
305	Arrow Blue
376	Petrol Blue Metallic
408	Bitter Chocolate
443	Copper Brown Metallic
451	Mocha Brown
463	Casablanca Beige Metallic
464	Tobacco Metallic
502	Cashmere Beige
601	Lilac
655	Platinum Metallic (Special)
700	Black
708	Black Metallic
908	Grand Prix White
936	Silver Metallic

Interior

Leatherette (vinyl) standard:
> Beige, Brown, or Blue

Leather, optional:
> Beige, Yellow, Dark Green, Dark Blue, Blue, Cork, Black, Brown, Light Red, White, or Doric Gray (Special)

Additional no-cost options:

Checkerboard velour:

Beige/Brown, Blue/Black, Brown/Black, or Gray/Black

Note: All of the above interiors were available on Turbo models except leatherette. The Turbo also continued the Tartan Dress Plaid option.

Carpets:

Cut-pile velour:

Beige, Brown, Dark Blue, Dark Green, Yellow, Cork, Red, or Black

Options See note and listing for 1978 model year

1980 only:

M439   *Weissach Limited Edition* 911SC. Number of cars built for the United States: 408. Choice of Black Metallic or Platinum Metallic exterior over Doric Gray full leather interior with Burgundy piping. Other options included in this package: whale-tail rear spoiler, flexible rubber lip for front spoiler, passenger-side external mirror, power sunroof, foglights, power antenna, door-mounted radio speakers, dual radio speakers in rear package shelf, Bilstein shocks, 6Jx15 Fuchs alloys in front and 7Jx15 in rear with Pirelli CN36 185/70R15 and 215/60R15 tires, and wheel centers painted Platinum Metallic.

B Program – Produced from August 1980 to July 1981

Model	Chassis Serial No.	Engine Serial No.	Produced
911SC	WPOZZZ91ZBS100001–3181	6310001–on (930/10)	3,181
911SC Targa	WPOZZZ91ZBS140001–1703		1,703
911SC U.S.	WPOAA091CBS120001–1573	6410001–on (930/16)	1,573
911SC U.S. Targa	WPOAA091CBS160001–1407		1,407
911SC Japan	WPOZZZ91ZBS129501–9622	6318001–on (930/17)	122
911SC Japan Targa	WPOZZZ91ZBS169501–9510		10
Turbo	WPOZZZ93ZBS000001–698	6710001–on (930/60)	698
Turbo Canada	WPOJAO93-BS050001-0063		63

1981 was the first model year that used the 17-digit international standard chassis serial number. These serial numbers can be broken down as follows: WPO = the world manufacturer's code for Porsche. The fourth letter was the body code for the United States and Canada (A = Coupe, E = Targa, J = Turbo) or a "Z" for the RoW. The fifth letter signified an engine version for the United States. The sixth letter was only for U.S. cars and shows if the car was equipped with seatbelts only (0) or airbags (2). The next two digits were model type, 91 = 911 and

93 = 930 (Turbo). The next letter or number was a placeholder; on U.S. cars the "C" shown above could be a number from 0 to 9 or an "X." The twelfth letter was the model year, B = 1981. The following letter was the manufacturing plant of origin, S = Stuttgart. The next number was the continuation of the model type, for example, 91 (seventh and eighth characters in serial number) plus 1 = 911, 93 plus 0 = 930. The thirteenth number designated body and engine. The last four digits, as before, were the individual build numbers in sequence. Note that "Z" is used merely as a placeholder to conform to the 17-digit standard.

Engines

Type 930/10 fitted to RoW 911SC. Same as 930/09 except:

Compression ratio 9.8:1

Fuel requirement raised to 98 RON

204 horsepower @ 5,900 rpm

189 foot-pounds torque @ 4,200 rpm

Type 930/16 fitted to U.S. and Canada 911SC. Same as 930/07

Type 930/17 fitted to Japan 911SC. Same as 930/08

Type 930/60 fitted to RoW and Canada Turbos. Same as prior year

Racing Engines

Type 935/75 2.7 936 Turbo

92.3-millimeter bore x 66-millimeter stroke

2.7-liter, 2,650 cc

7.0:1 compression ratio

600 horsepower @ 8,200 rpm, 1.4 bar boost

Type 930/81 3.2 935 Turbo

Same as 930/80

760 horsepower @ 7,800 rpm, 1.4 bar boost

Transmissions

Same as prior year

Exterior
Standard Colors

Color Code	Color Name
20A	Mint Green
20C	Moss Green Metallic
027	Guards Red
30T	Light Blue Metallic
31G	Pacific Blue Metallic
304	Minerva Blue Metallic
305	Arrow Blue
451	Mocha Brown
474	Rosewood Metallic
523	Bamboo
524	Caramel

Color Code	Color Name *(continued)*
700	Black
708	Black Metallic
895	Wine Red Metallic
908	Grand Prix White
956	Zinc Metallic

Interior
Leatherette (vinyl) standard:
    Beige, Brown, Blue, or Black
Leather, optional:
    Beige, Mint Green, Dark Blue, Hannibal Gray, Black, Brown,
    Red, or Papyrus White
Additional no-cost options:
    Checkerboard velour:
        Beige/Brown, Blue/Black, or Gray/Black
    Berber tweed:
        Beige, Blue/Black, or Gray/Black
Note: All of the above interiors were available on Turbo models, except
leatherette. Turbo also continues the Tartan Dress Plaid option.
Carpets:
    Cut-pile velour:
        Beige, Brown, Dark Blue, Mint Green, or Black

Options See note and listing for 1978 model year
Sonderwunsch   Special order conversion; first slant-nose Turbo
    delivered July 1981. Only one delivered as 1981 model.

C Program – Produced from August 1981 to July 1982

Model	Chassis Serial No.	Engine Serial No.	Produced
911SC	WPOZZZ91ZCS100001–3307	63C0001–on (930/10)	3,307
911SC Targa	WPOZZZ91ZCS140001–1737		1,737
911SC U.S.	WPOAAO91CCS120001–2457	64C0001–on (930/16)	2,457
911SC Targa U.S.	WPOEAO91CCS160001–2426		2,426
911SC Japan	WPOZZZ91ZCS109501–9628	63C8001–on (930/17)	128
911SC Targa Japan	WPOZZZ91CS149501–9562		62
Turbo	WPOZZZ93ZCS000001–938	67C0001–on (930/60)	938
Turbo Canada	WPOJAO93CCS050001–0089		89

    The only change to the serial number from 1981 was that the
10th letter is now "C" to designate the model year 1982.

Engines

Type 930/10 fitted to RoW 911SC. Same as prior year
Type 930/16 fitted to U.S. and Canada 911SC. Same as prior year
Type 930/17 fitted to Japan 911SC. Same as prior year
Type 930/60 fitted to RoW and Canada Turbos. Same as prior year

Racing Engines

Type 935/75 2.7 936 Turbo
      92.3-millimeter bore x 66-millimeter stroke
      2.7-liter, 2,650 cc
      7.0:1 compression ratio
      600 horsepower @ 8,200 rpm, 1.4 bar boost
Type 930/81 3.2 935 Turbo. Same as 930/80
      760 horsepower @ 7,800 rpm, 1.4 bar boost

Transmissions

Same as prior year

Exterior
Standard Colors

Color Code	Color Name
20A	Mint Green
20C	Moss Green Metallic
027	Guards Red
30T	Light Blue Metallic
31G	Pacific Blue Metallic
304	Minerva Blue Metallic
305	Arrow Blue
451	Mocha Brown
474	Rosewood Metallic
523	Bamboo
524	Caramel
655	Platinum Metallic
700	Black
708	Black Metallic
895	Wine Red Metallic
908	Grand Prix White
956	Zinc Metallic
961	Meteor Metallic (Special)

Interior

Leatherette (vinyl) standard:
      Beige, Brown, Blue, or Black
Leather, optional:
      Beige, Mint Green, Dark Blue, Hannibal Gray, Black, Brown,
      Red, Papyrus White, or Burgundy (Special)

Additional no-cost options:
  Checkerboard velour:
    Beige/Brown, Blue/Black, or Gray/Black
  Berber tweed:
    Beige, Blue/Black, or Gray/Black
Note: All of the above interiors were available on Turbo models.
Carpets:
  Same as 1981 plus Burgundy (Special model)

Options
See note and listing for 1978 model year
Ferry Porsche Edition A total of 200 cars with the Special Meteor
    Metallic exterior and Burgundy leather interior. "Ferry
    Porsche" signature on headrests. Color-coded 7Jx15 front, and
    8Jx15 rear, Fuchs alloy wheels with 185/70VR15 and
    215/60VR15 tires.
Slant-nose Turbos A total of 38 cars delivered as special orders in 1982.

D Program – Produced from August 1982 to July 1983

Model	Chassis Serial No.	Engine Serial No.	Produced
911SC	WPOZZZ91ZDS100001–2995	63D0001–on (930/10)	2,995
911SC Targa	WPOZZZ91ZDS140001–1258		1,258
911SC Cabriolet	WPOZZZ91ZDS150001–2406		2,406
911SC U.S.	WPOAA091CDS120001–2599	64D0001–on (930/16)	2,599
911SC Targa U.S.	WPOEA091CDS160001–1430		1,430
911SC Cabriolet U.S.	WPOEA091CDS170001–1718		1,718
911SC Japan	WPOZZZ91ZDS109501–9645	63D8001–on (930/17)	145
911SC Targa Japan	WPOZZZ91ZDS149501–9562		62
Turbo	WPOZZZ93ZDS000001–1015	67D0001–on (930/66)	1,015
Turbo Canada	WPOJAO93CDS050001–0065		65

The only change to the serial number from 1981 was that the
10th letter is now "D" to designate the model year 1983. The letter
"E" in U.S. cars' serial numbers indicated either a Targa or Cabriolet
with the introduction of the latter during 1983.

Engines

Normally aspirated same as 1982 models

Type 930/66. Same as 930/60 except:

    Revised exhaust with wastegate vented to the outside air

    Same horsepower rating as 930/60

    321 foot-pounds torque @ 4,000 rpm

Racing Engines

Type 930/18 3.0 RS

    3.0-liter, 2,994 cc

    10.3:1 compression ratio

    Kugelfischer mechanical fuel injection

    255 horsepower @ 7,000 rpm

    184 foot-pounds torque @ 6,500 rpm

Transmissions

Same as 1982 models

Exterior
Standard Colors

Color Code	Color Name
20A	Mint Green
20C	Moss Green Metallic
027	Guards Red
32Z	Glacier Blue
182	Chiffon White
655	Pewter Metallic
661	Slate Blue Metallic
662	Quartz Gray Metallic
700	Black
708	Black Metallic
810	Ruby Red Metallic

1981 U.S. cars (like this 911SC Targa) stayed at 180 horsepower for 1981 while RoW cars climbed from 188 to 204 horsepower.

The debut of the first 911 Cabriolet model, the SC Cabriolet was in 1983.

Color Code	Color Name *(continued)*
811	Kiln Red Metallic
908	Grand Prix White
956	Zinc Metallic
966	Light Bronze Metallic

Interior
Leatherette (vinyl) standard:
>Burgundy, Brown, Blue, or Black

Leather, optional:
>Gray Beige, Dark Green, Blue, Champagne, Black, Brown, Red, Pearl White, or Burgundy

Additional no-cost options:
>Checkerboard velour:
>>Brown/Gray, Blue/Gray, Light Gray/Black, or Burgundy/Gray

>Berber tweed:
>>Beige/Brown, Blue/Black, Gray/Black, Burgundy/Gray, or Gray Beige/Gray

>Wavy Stitch cloth:
>>Brown, Blue, Black, Gray Beige, or Burgundy

Note: All of the above interiors were available on Turbo models.
Carpets:
>Cut-pile velour:
>>Light Gray, Brown, Dark Blue, Dark Green, Black, Gray Beige, Red, Burgundy, or Champagne

Options
See note and listing for 1978 model year
Slant-nose Turbos Special order conversions. In 1983, 35 of these cars were delivered.

Chapter Eight

1984–1989, Carrera 3.2

1984: The Carrera replaced the 911SC. A new 3.2-liter engine combined the 95-millimeter-bore Nikasil cylinders of the SC with the 74.4 stroke of the Turbo crankshaft to arrive at its displacement. A Bosch Motronic 2 DME (Digital Motor Electronics) engine management system was fitted along with LE-Jetronic fuel injection. Improved oil-fed chain tensioners were another major development on this engine.

Bodywork on the new Carrera was similar to the SC with a new front spoiler that had integrated fog lights. Larger and thicker brake discs were fitted front and rear (11.8-inch-diameter front disc, 12.1-inch rear) along with the power brake booster from the Turbo. A brake pad warning indicator was added to the instrument panel.

Standard wheels and tires were 6Jx15 with 185/70 tires in front and 7Jx15 with 215/60 tires in the rear. Optional were 7Jx16 wheels with 205/55ZR tires up front and 8Jx16 wheels and 225/50 ZR tires at the rear.

The Turbo engine was fitted with the upgraded chain tensioners. The Turbo was also equipped with the dash-mounted brake pad warning indicator and a new heater system with three-speed fan.

Option M491 was a Turbo Look package for Carrera coupes that consisted of front and rear fenders, rear fender flares, and front and rear spoilers identical to the Turbo. Also included in the Turbo Look were the front hubs, rear torsion bar tube, suspension arms, and brake system of the Turbo. Wheels measured 7Jx16 with 205/55VR16 tires up front and 8Jx16 with 225/50VR16 tires at the rear.

Prices were (in U.S. dollars): coupe, $31,960; Targa, $32,450; and Cabriolet, $36,450.

1985: A four-spoke, leather-wrapped steering wheel became standard. The radio antenna was embedded in the windshield. A finned oil cooler was added in the right front fender. Improvements were made to the shifter. Boge dual-tube "GZ" gas-pressure shocks became standard equipment. Porsche introduced its first power adjustable seats.

The Turbo Look option was available on the Targa and Cabriolet as well as the coupe. Electrically heated windshield washer nozzles and Sekuriflex safety windshield were available as options.

In addition to new seats and radio antenna placement in the windshield, Turbo standard equipment included central locking, heated seats, a larger brake master cylinder, and larger anti-roll bars (22 millimeter front, 20 millimeter rear).

1986: Front seats were lowered by 20 millimeters and sport seats were a no-cost option. A new dash panel had larger air vents than the previous model. Sun visors were fitted with vanity mirrors with sliding covers. A new cabin heat temperature sensor was fitted. Carrera models came equipped with larger anti-roll bars: 22 millimeters in front, 21 millimeters rear. The rear torsion bars also enlarged from 24 millimeters to 25 millimeters in diameter. U.S. cars featured a third brake light mounted at the top of the rear window. Options included a power top for the Cabriolet and a 10 percent shorter gear shift on all models.

The Turbo model returned to the U.S. market equipped with DME, oxygen sensors, and catalytic converters to meet emissions and fuel requirements. Rear wheels were increased on all Turbo models to 9Jx16 with 245/45VR tires.

U.S. prices were: Turbo, $48,000; Carrera coupe, $31,950; Targa, $33,450; and Cabriolet, $36,450.

1987: The Type 915 transmission was replaced by the Getrag-built G50 five-speed with Borg-Warner synchromesh. Reverse gear selection was revised to move to the left and forward. The clutch size was enlarged to 240 millimeters, same as the Turbo, and hydraulically actuated.

U.S., Canada, and Japan engines were remapped for more horsepower (217 horsepower) and furnished with a thermostatically controlled fan for the front oil cooler. Australia received its first unique model, with 207 horsepower.

The rear reflector strip between the taillights was revised to include the back-up lights and dual rear fog lights. The U.S. center-mounted brake light was moved to the bottom of the rear window. U.S.-legal headlights took on the appearance of RoW units. Standard wheel sizes remained the same but front tires were changed to 195/65VR15.

A power top was made standard equipment on the Cabriolet. Targas received improved weather sealing.

Turbos were available as Cabriolet and Targa for the first time. The 930S, the official factory Turbo slant-nose option for the United States, became available in March 1987. The slant-nose option featured steel front bodywork consisting of flat fenders with retractable headlights, vents along the fender tops, rocker panel fairings, air

The first year for Carrera 3.2 models was 1984. "Phone dial" wheels were standard in most markets.

intakes in the rear fenders with side strakes, an oil cooler with fan at the rear air inlet, and Bridgestone RE71 tires. European models included a 330-horsepower engine.

1988: Standard-equipment wheels changed from cast alloy "telephone dials" to Fuchs forged alloys. Size remained at 7Jx15 with 195/65VR15 tires (front) and 8Jx15 with 215/60VR15 tires (rear). The standard-equipment list now included items that were options in certain markets including: passenger-door mirror, passenger-side power seat, central locking, and headlight washers. All models also came with a leather-covered shifter and leather shifter boot.

Optional wheels were Fuchs forged alloys, 6Jx16 with 205/55VR16 tires (front), and 7Jx16 with 225/50VR16 tires (rear).

The Anniversary Carrera was offered in a limited production run to commemorate the 250,000th 911, which was made on June 3, 1987. Special Silver Blue exterior paint and a blue leather interior were used on the 875 cars produced. Of these, 300 went to the U.S.

1989: Standard wheels were 6Jx16 with 205/55ZR tires in front, and 8Jx16 with 225/50ZR tires in rear. The alarm system included flashing red LED lights in door lock buttons to indicate when the system is armed.

Options included a radio with CD player.

A Speedster model was made between January and September 1989. It featured a cut-down windshield frame, a lightweight convertible top, and humpback fiberglass covering over the rear seat area (rear seats were removed). Of the 2,065 made, 823 were delivered to the U.S. They were the last cars built at the old 911 body plant.

The Turbo was fitted with the five-speed G50 transmission and hydraulic clutch. It also received larger anti-roll bars: 22 millimeter front, 18 millimeter rear.

U.S. prices: Speedster, $65,480. Turbo—coupe, $70,975; Targa, $77,065; Cabriolet $85,060. Carrera—coupe, $51,205; Targa, $52,435; Cabriolet $59,200.

Competition/Sport: The Club Sport version of Carrera, the M637 Sport Package, included a higher engine rev limit, sport shocks, stiffer engine mounts, and 7J/8Jx16 wheels. Deletion of equipment and interior trim brought the weight down from 2,665 pounds to 2,555 pounds. It is believed that, out of 340 made from September 1987 until September 1989, 28 of these cars came to the United States.

Dimensions	**1984–89**
Wheelbase:	89.4 inches
Height:	52.8 inches
Width:	65 inches
Weight, 911	2,670 pounds
Weight, Turbo:	2,940 pounds
Fuel tank capacity	21.0 gallons

E Program – Produced from August 1983 to July 1984

Model	Chassis Serial No.	Engine Serial No.	Produced
Carrera	WPOZZZ91ZES100001–4033	63E00001–on (930/20)	4,033
Carrera Targa	WPOZZZ91ZES140001–1469		1,469
Carrera Cabrio	WPOZZZ91ZES150001–1835		1,835
Carrera Japan	WPOZZZ91ZES109501–9717	64E00001–on (930/21)	217
Carrera Targa Japan	WPOZZZ91ZES149501–9564		64
Carrera Cabrio Japan	WPOZZZ91ZES159501–9577		77
Carrera U.S.	WPOABO91CES120001–2282		2,282
Carrera Targa U.S.	WPOEBO91CES160001–2260		2,260
Carrera Cabrio U.S.	WPOEBO91CES170001–1191		1,191
Turbo	WPOZZZ93ZES000001–0804	67E001–on (930/66)	804
Turbo Canada	WPOJAO93CES050001–0077		77

The only change from 1983 is that the 10th digit in the serial number becomes "E" to designate a 1984 model.

Engines

Type 930/20 fitted to RoW Carrera

> 95-millimeter bore x 74.4-millimeter stroke
>
> 3.2-liter, 3,164 cc
>
> Digital Motor Electronic, DME (Motronic 2) engine manage ment system
>
> Bosch LE-Jetronic fuel injection
>
> Oil-fed chain tensioners
>
> Crankshaft similar to turbo engine
>
> Compression ratio of 10.3:1
>
> Fuel requirement leaded 98 RON
>
> 231 horsepower @ 5,900 rpm
>
> 209 foot-pounds torque @ 4,800 rpm

Type 930/21 fitted to U.S., Canada, Japan Carrera. Same as 930/20 except:

> Compression ratio of 9.5:1
>
> Fuel requirement unleaded 91 RON
>
> 207 horsepower @ 5,900 rpm
>
> 192 foot-pounds torque @ 4,800 rpm

Type 930/66 fitted to RoW and Canada Turbo. Same as prior year

Transmissions
Type 915/67 five-speed manual fitted to RoW Carrera
Type 915/68 five-speed manual fitted to U.S., Canada, Japan
Carrera
Type 930/34 four-speed manual fitted to all Turbos

Exterior
Standard Colors

Color Code	Color
027	Guards Red
32Z	Glacier Blue
182	Chiffon White
700	Black
908	Grand Prix White

Special Order Colors

Color Code	Color
20C	Moss Green Metallic
655	Pewter Metallic
661	Slate Blue Metallic
662	Quartz Gray Metallic
810	Ruby Red Metallic
811	Kiln Red Metallic
956	Zinc Metallic
966	Light Bronze Metallic

Interior
Leatherette (vinyl) standard:
 Gray Beige, Burgundy, Cadbury Brown, Blue, Black
Leather, optional:
 Gray Beige, Dark Green, Blue, Champagne, Black, Cadbury
  Brown, Can-Can Red, Pearl White, and Burgundy

The 1985 Carrera 3.2 Cabriolet with Turbo Look, which became an option package for Targa and Cabriolet models that year.

Additional no-cost options:

Checkerboard velour:

Brown/Gray, Blue/Gray, Light Gray/Black, Burgundy/Gray

Pinstripe velour:

Beige/Brown, Black/White, Gray/Black, Burgundy/White, Gray Beige/White, Blue/White

Wavy Stitch cloth:

Brown, Blue, Black, Gray Beige, Burgundy

"Porsche" script diagonal pattern cloth:

Black, Brown, Gray Beige, Blue, Burgundy

Note: All of the above interiors were available on Turbo models.

Carpets:

Cut-pile velour:

Light Gray, Brown, Dark Blue, Dark Green, Black, Gray Beige, Can-Can Red, Burgundy, Champagne

Options

See note and listing for 1978 model year

M491   The *"Turbo Look"* option was available on the Carrera Coupe. This included flared front and rear fenders; rear wing and front spoiler of Turbo models, plus the suspension, brakes, and 7-inch front and 9-inch rear wheels of the Turbos.

Slant-nose Turbos   Special conversions, 34 cars delivered in 1984.

F Program – Produced from August 1984 to July 1985

Model	Chassis Serial No.	Engine Serial No.	Produced
Carrera	WPOZZZ91ZFS100001–3529	63F00001–on (930/20)	3,529
Carrera Targa	WPOZZZ91ZFS140001–1435		1,435
Carrera Cabrio	WPOZZZ91ZFS150001–1583		1,583
Carrera Japan	WPOZZZ91ZFS109501–9722	64F00001–on (930/21)	222
Carrera Targa Japan	WPOZZZ91ZFS149501–9564		64
Carrera Cabrio Japan	WPOZZZ91ZFS159501–9575		75
Carrera U.S.	WPOABO91CFS120001–1959		1,959
Carrera Targa U.S.	WPOEBO91CFS160001–1942		1,942
Carrera Cabrio U.S.	WPOEBO91CFS170001–1050		1,050
Turbo	WPOZZZ93ZFS000001–1063	67F001–on (930/66)	1.063
Turbo Canada	WPOJAO93CFS050001–0085		85

The only change from 1983 was that the 10th digit in the serial number became "F" to designate a 1985 model.

Porsche extended its guarantee against rust perforation of body parts to 10 years beginning with the 1986 model.

Engines
Same as 1984
Type 930/21 for Austria, Australia, and Switzerland was equipped with a catalytic converter and oxygen sensor. Optional for Germany (Option M298)

Transmissions
Type 915/72 (w/oil cooler) five-speed manual for all noncatalyst engines
Type 915/73 (w/o oil cooler) five-speed manual for catalyst-equipped engines
Type 930/34 fitted to Turbos as 1984

Exterior
Standard Colors

Color Code	Color
027	Guards Red
347	Dark Blue
536	Pastel Beige
673	Marble Gray
700	Black
908	Grand Prix White

Special Order Colors

Color Code	Color
20C	Moss Green Metallic
33N	Crystal Green Metallic
33P	Iris Blue Metallic
33X	Prussian Blue Metallic
492	Nutmeg Brown Metallic
539	White Gold Metallic
822	Garnet Red Metallic
936	Silver Metallic
961	Meteor Metallic

The 1987 Turbo shows off a dual outlet exhaust and a deeper rear wing to cover the intercooler.

Interior

Leatherette (vinyl) standard:
> Gray Green, Burgundy, Cadbury Brown, Blue, Black

Leather, optional:
> Gray Green, Dark Green, Blue, Champagne, Black, Cadbury Brown, Can-Can Red, Pearl White, Wild Buffalo, Ocean Blue, and Burgundy

Additional no-cost options:
> Pinstripe velour:
>> Brown/White, Black/White, Burgundy/White, Gray Green/White, Blue/White

> Pinstripe flannel:
>> Brown, Blue, Black, Gray Green, Burgundy

> "Porsche" script diagonal pattern cloth:
>> Black, Brown, Gray Green, Blue, Burgundy

Note: All of the above interiors were available on Turbo models.

Carpets:
> Cut-pile velour:
>> Light Gray, Brown, Dark Blue, Dark Green, Black, Gray Green, Can-Can Red, Burgundy, Champagne, White

Cabriolet top:
> Black, Dark Brown, Dark Blue, Burgundy, Gray Green

Options

See note and listing for 1978 model year

"Turbo Look"   Option available on Carrera Targas and Cabriolets as well as Coupes

Slant-nose Turbos   Special order conversions, 44 models delivered in 1985.

G Program – Produced from August 1985 to July 1986

Model	Chassis Serial No.	Engine Serial No.	Produced
Carrera	WPOZZZ91ZGS100001–4031	63G00001–on (930/20)	4,031
Carrera Targa	WPOZZZ91ZGS140001–1758		1,758
Carrera Cabrio	WPOZZZ91ZGS150001–2358		2,358
Carrera Japan	WPOZZZ91ZGS109501–9733	64G00001–on (930/21)	233
Carrera Targa Japan	WPOZZZ91ZGS149501–9579		79
Carrera Cabrio Japan	WPOZZZ91ZGS159501–9580		80
Carrera U.S.	WPOABO91CGS120001–2619		2,19
Carrera Targa U.S.	WPOEBO91CGS160001–1976		1,976
Carrera Cabrio U.S.	WPOEBO91CGS170001–1986		1,986
Turbo	WPOZZZ93ZGS000001–1158	67G001–on (930/66)	1,158
Turbo Canada	WPOJAO93CGS050001–0088		88
Turbo U.S.	WPOJBO93CGS050001–1424	930/68	1,424

The only change from 1983 was that the 10th digit in the serial number became "G" to designate a 1986 model.

The 1987 Targa with a revised rear reflector incorporating back-up lights and dual rear fog lights.

Engines
Type 930/20 fitted to RoW Carreras identical to 1985
Type 930/21 fitted to U.S., Canada, and Japan Carreras identical
       to 1985
Type 930/66 fitted to RoW Turbos identical to 1985
Type 930/68 fitted to U.S. Turbo. Same as 930/66 except :
       Digital Motor Electronics (DME) engine management system
       Oxygen sensor (Lambda sonde) with catalytic converters
       Unleaded fuel requirement, 96 RON
       282 horsepower @ 5,500 rpm
       287 foot-pounds torque @ 4,000 rpm

Transmissions
Type 915/72 five-speed manual fitted to RoW Carreras
Type 915/73 five-speed manual fitted to U.S., Canada, and Japan
       Carreras
Type 930/36 four-speed manual fitted to all Turbos

Exterior
Standard Colors (same as 1985)

Color Code	Color
027	Guards Red
347	Dark Blue
536	Pastel Beige
673	Marble Gray
700	Black
908	Grand Prix White

Special Order Colors (same as 1985)

Color Code	Color
20C	Moss Green Metallic
33N	Crystal Green Metallic
33P	Iris Blue Metallic
33X	Prussian Blue Metallic
492	Nutmeg Brown Metallic
539	White Gold Metallic
822	Garnet Red Metallic
936	Silver Metallic
961	Meteor Metallic

Interior
Leatherette (vinyl) standard:
       Gray Beige, Gray Green, Burgundy, Cadbury Brown, Blue, Black
Leather, optional:
       Gray Beige, Gray Green, Dark Green, Blue, Champagne, Black,
       Cadbury Brown, Can-Can Red, Pearl White, Wild Buffalo,
       Ocean Blue, and Burgundy

Additional no-cost options:
    Pinstripe velour:
        Gray Beige/White, Brown/White, Black/White,
        Burgundy/White, Gray Green/White, Blue/White
    Pinstripe flannel:
        Brown, Blue, Black, Gray Green, Burgundy
    "Porsche" script diagonal pattern cloth:
        Black, Brown, Gray Beige, Gray Green, Blue, Burgundy
Note: All of the above interiors were available on Turbo models.
Carpets:
    Cut-pile velour:
        Light Gray, Brown, Dark Blue, Dark Green, Black, Gray
        Green, Can-Can Red, Burgundy, Champagne, White, Gray Beige
    Cabriolet top:
        Black, Dark Brown, Dark Blue, Burgundy, Gray Green

Options
See note and listing for 1978 model year
"Turbo Look"   Option available on all models. Turbo Look cars
    called Carrera SE (Sport Equipment) in the United Kingdom.
Slant-nose Turbos   Special order conversions, 52 models delivered
    in 1986.

H Program – Produced from August 1986 to July 1987

Model	Chassis Serial No.	Engine Serial No.	Produced
Carrera	WPOZZZ91ZHS100001–3381	63H00001–on (930/20)	3,381
Club Sport	WPOZZZ91ZHS105001–5081		81
Carrera Targa	WPOZZZ91ZHS140001–1354		1,354
Carrera Cabrio	WPOZZZ91ZHS150001–1464		1,464
Carrera Japan	WPOZZZ91ZHS109501–9808	64H00001–on (930/25)	308
Carrera Targa Japan	WPOZZZ91ZHS149501–9579		79
Carrera Cabrio Japan	WPOZZZ91ZHS159501–9585		85
Carrera U.S.	WPOABO91CHS120001–2916		2,916
Club Sport U.S.	WPOABO91CHS125001–5300		300
Carrera Targa U.S.	WPOEBO91CHS160001–2232		2,232
Carrera Cabrio U.S.	WPOEBO91CHS170001–2653		2,653

Model	Chassis Serial No.	Engine Serial No.	Produced
Turbo	WPOZZZ93ZHS000001–0720	67H001–on (930/66)	1,158
Turbo Canada	WPOJAO93CHS050001–0088		88
Turbo Cabrio	WPOZZZ93ZHS020001–0142		142
Turbo Cabrio U.S.	WPOEBO93CHS070001–0183	68H001–on (930/68)	183
Turbo Targa	WPOZZZ93ZHS010001–0069		69
Turbo Targa U.S.	WPOEBO93CHS060001–0087		87
Turbo Slant-Nose	WPOZZZ93ZHS050001–0087		87
Turbo S/N Targa	WPOZZZ93ZHS060001–0087		87
Turbo S/N Cabrio	WPOZZZ93ZHS070001–0087		87
Turbo S/N U.S.	WPOEBO93CHS050001–0087		87
Turbo S/N Targa U.S.	WPOEBO93CHS060001–0087		87
Turbo S/N Cabrio U.S.	WPOEBO93CHS070001–0087		87

The only change from 1983 was that the 10th digit in the serial number became "H" to designate a 1987 model. Porsche also produced the 959 coupe as a special 1987 model. Serial numbers for the 959 run from WPOZZZ95ZHS900001 to WPOZZZ95ZHS900254.

Engines

Porsche established a policy that all engines would produce similar power no matter what the emissions or fuel standards may be for a country. While there are two major engine types, six different DME control units were used to carry out this policy.

Type 930/20 fitted to RoW Carreras except Switzerland
Compression ratio 10.3:1
Fuel requirement is 98 with or without lead
No catalytic converters
231 horsepower @ 5,900 rpm
209 foot-pounds torque @ 4,800 rpm

Type 930/21 fitted to Australia Carreras. Similar to 1986 U.S. engine except:
Fuel requirement 91 RON unleaded
207 horsepower @ 5,900 rpm
192 foot-pounds torque @ 4,800 rpm

Type 930/25 fitted to Carreras for U.S., Canada, Japan, and European countries without premium grade unleaded fuel. Similar

to 930/21 with remapped DME except:
>Compression ratio 9.5:1
>Catalytic converters
>Fuel requirement 95 RON unleaded
>217 horsepower @ 5,900 rpm
>195 foot-pounds torque @ 4,800 rpm

Type 930/26 fitted to Swiss Carreras. Similar to 930/20 except:
>Compression ratio 9.5:1
>No catalytic converters but auxiliary air injection
>Extra noise reducing equipment
>Fuel requirement 98 RON, leaded or unleaded
>231 horsepower @ 5,900 rpm
>195 foot-pounds torque @ 4,800 rpm

DME control units for above engines:
>911.618.111.12 high compression engines, worldwide
>911.618.111.13 countries with low octane fuel
>911.618.111.14 U.S., Japan, Canada, Austria, Switzerland, and RoW w/catalytic converters
>911.618.111.15 high compression engines with sport package (Club Sport) that increased rev limit to 6,840 rpm
>911.618.111.16 low octane fuel engines with sport package
>911.618.111.17 U.S., Canada, Japan, etc., with sport package

Turbo engines same as 1986 model year

The 959 used a 450-horsepower, 2.85-liter engine with water-cooled four-valve cylinder heads, air-cooled cylinders, two sequential turbochargers, and a special Bosch MP-Jetronic fuel injection system.

Transmissions

Type 950/00 five-speed manual fitted to RoW Carreras
>New transmission, Getrag model G50
>Fully synchronized reverse gear, now to the left and forward
>Hydraulic clutch

Type 950/01 five-speed manual fitted to U.S., Canada, Japan Carreras
>Same as Type 950/00 except for gear ratios

Type 930/36 four-speed manual fitted to all Turbos

Exterior
Standard Colors

Color Code	Color
10W	Summer Yellow
21M	Turquoise
027	Guards Red
80F	Carmine Red
347	Dark Blue
499	Caramel Beige
700	Black
908	Grand Prix White

Special Order Colors

Color Code	Color
35U	Venetian Blue Metallic
35V	Marine Blue Metallic
35Y	Lagoon Green Metallic
40B	Nougat Brown Metallic
40D	Espresso Brown Metallic
80D	Cassis Red Metallic
697	Diamond Blue Metallic
699	Granite Green Metallic
980	Silver Metallic

Interior

Leatherette (vinyl) standard:
> Gray Green, Burgundy, Linen, Mahogany, Blue, Black

Leather, optional:
> Gray Green, Blue, Champagne, Black, Brown, Plum Red, Linen, Silver Gray, Caramel, Burgundy, Venetian Blue, and Mahogany

Additional no-cost options:
> Pinstripe velour:
>> Mahogany/White, Black/White, Burgundy/White, Gray Green/White, Blue/White
>
> Pinstripe flannel:
>> Mahogany, Anthracite, Blue, Gray Green, Burgundy
>
> "Porsche" script diagonal pattern cloth:
>> Black, Mahogany, Gray Beige, Gray Green, Blue, Burgundy

Note: All of the above interiors were available on Turbo models.

Carpets:
> Cut-pile velour:
>> Silver Gray, Mahogany, Blue, Linen, Black, Gray Green, Plum Red, Burgundy, Champagne, Caramel, Venetian Blue
>
> Cabriolet top:
>> Black, Mahogany, Blue, Burgundy, Gray Green

The 1988 Targa—standard wheels changed from phone dials to Fuchs rims.

Options

See note and listing for 1978 model year

"Turbo Look"   Option available on all models. Turbo Look cars called Carrera SE (Sport Equipment) in the United Kingdom.

Slant-nose Turbos   Special order conversions, 33 models delivered in 1987.

M506 *Slant-nose Turbo*   Became regular production option. Called Turbo SE (Special Equipment) in the United Kingdom. In the United States, this model was called the 930S and became available starting in March 1987.

M637 *Carrera Club Sport*   This option deleted items like power windows, power seats, rear wiper, central locking, radio, passenger sun visor, rear seats, sound insulation, air conditioning, and undercoating to save approximately 110 pounds. A short-throw shifter was added. The engine redline was increased from 6520 rpm to 6840 rpm with a different computer chip for the DME. Bilstein sport shocks were also added. Wheels were 6Jx15 front, and 7Jx15 rear with Pirelli P6 tires sized 195/65VR15 and 215/60VR15 respectively. This was later changed to 16-inch wheels of the same width with Dunlop D40 tires measuring 205/55VR16 and 225/50VR16.

J Program – Produced from August 1987 to July 1988

Model	Chassis Serial No.	Engine Serial No.	Produced
Carrera	WPOZZZ91ZJS100001–3381	63J00001–on (930/20)	3,381
Club Sport	WPOZZZ91ZJS105001–5081		81
Carrera Targa	WPOZZZ91ZJS140001–1354		1,354
Carrera Cabrio	WPOZZZ91ZJS150001–1464		1,464
Carrera Japan	WPOZZZ91ZJS109501–9808	64J00001–on (930/25)	308
Carrera Targa Japan	WPOZZZ91ZJS149501–9579		79
Carrera Cabrio Japan	WPOZZZ91ZJS159501–9585		85
Carrera U.S.	WPOABO91CJS120001–2916		2,916
Club Sport U.S.	WPOABO91CJS125001–5300		300
Carrera Targa U.S.	WPOEBO91CJS160001–2232		2,232
Carrera Cabrio U.S.	WPOEBO91CJS170001–2653		2,653
Turbo	WPOZZZ93ZJS000001–0677	67J001–on (930/66)	677
Turbo Cabrio	WPOZZZ93ZJS020001–0242		242

Model	Chassis Serial No.	Engine Serial No.	Produced
Turbo Targa	WPOZZZ93ZJS010001–0136		136
Turbo U.S./Canada	WPOJBO93CJS050001–0701	68J001–on (930/68)	701
Turbo Cabrio U.S./Canada	WPOEBO93CJS070001–0591		591
Turbo Targa U.S./Canada	WPOEBO93CJS060001–0141		141
Turbo Slant-Nose	WPOZZZ93ZJS050001–0591		591
Turbo S/N Targa N.A.[1]	WPOEBO93CJS060001–0591		591
Turbo S/N Cabrio N.A.	WPOEBO93CJS070001–0591		591
Turbo S/N U.S.	WPOEBO93CJS050001–0591		591

[1] N.A. stands for North America. Canada and the U.S. were combined.

The only change from 1983 was that the 10th digit in the serial number became "J" to designate a 1988 model.

Engines
Types 930/20, 930/25, and 930/26 carried over from 1987 model year
Types 930/66 and 930/68 Turbo engines carried over from 1987 model year

Transmissions
Type 950/00 and 950/01 were renamed G50/00 and G50/01, but otherwise remained the same as the 1987 model year.

The last year for the Carrera 3.2 was 1989. It was also the first year for standard 16-inch wheels (6J front, 8J rear).

Exterior
Standard Colors (same as 1987)

Color Code	Color
10W	Summer Yellow
21M	Turquoise
027	Guards Red
80F	Carmine Red
347	Dark Blue
499	Caramel Beige
700	Black
908	Grand Prix White

Special Order Colors (same as 1987)

Color Code	Color
35U	Venetian Blue Metallic
35V	Marine Blue Metallic
35Y	Lagoon Green Metallic
40B	Nougat Brown Metallic
40D	Espresso Brown Metallic
80D	Cassis Red Metallic
697	Diamond Blue Metallic
699	Granite Green Metallic
980	Silver Metallic

Interior
Leatherette (vinyl) standard:
    Gray Green, Burgundy, Linen, Mahogany, Blue, Black
Leather, optional:
    Gray Green, Blue, Champagne, Black, Brown, Plum Red,
        Linen, Silver Gray, Caramel, Burgundy, Venetian Blue,
        and Mahogany
Additional no-cost options:
    Pinstripe velour:
        Mahogany/White, Black/White, Burgundy/White, Gray
        Green/White, Blue/White
    Pinstripe flannel:
        Mahogany, Anthracite, Blue, Gray Green, Burgundy
        "Porsche" script diagonal pattern cloth:
        Black, Mahogany, Gray Beige, Gray Green, Blue, Burgundy
Note: All of the above interiors were available on Turbo models.
Carpets:
    Cut-pile velour:
        Silver Gray, Mahogany, Blue, Linen, Black, Gray Green,
        Plum Red, Burgundy, Champagne, Caramel, Venetian Blue
Cabriolet top:
    Black, Mahogany, Blue, Burgundy, Gray Green

Options

See note and listing for 1978 model year

M637 *Carrera Club Sport*   Discontinued after September 1989. A total of 340 cars were so equipped including 28 U.S. cars and 50 for the United Kingdom. All were coupes except for one special order Targa. Most were Grand Prix White. A "Carrera CS" decal in script for the sides was optional in the United Kingdom. For the United States and Germany a "CS" fender decal was an option instead of the side script. Wheel centers were red, white, or black.

Anniversary Carrera   Commemorated 25 years of 911 production. The exterior was Marine Blue Metallic with a blue metallic leather interior featuring an "F. Porsche" signature on the headrests. Carpeting was Silver Blue silk velour. There was no external identification, but the cars did have an "anniversary" dash plaque. A total of 875 cars were produced, and 300 came to the United States—120 Coupes, 100 Cabriolets, and 80 Targas.

K Program – Produced from August 1988 to July 1989

Model	Chassis Serial No.	Engine Serial No.	Produced
Carrera	WPOZZZ91ZKS100001–3532	63K00001–on (930/20)	3,532
Carrera Targa	WPOZZZ91ZKS140001–1063		1,063
Carrera Cabrio	WPOZZZ91ZKS150001–2787		2,787
Club Sport	WPOZZZ91ZKS105001–5090		90
Speedster	WPOZZZ91ZKS153000–4242		1,242
Carrera 4[2]	WPOZZZ96ZKS400001–2068	62K00001–on (M64/01)	2,068
Carrera U.S.	WPOABO91CKS120001–1156	64K00001–on (930/25)	1,156
Carrera Targa U.S.	WPOEBO91CKS160001–0860		860
Carrera Cabrio U.S.	WPOEBO91CKS170001–1361		1,361
Speedster U.S.	WPOEBO91CKS173001–0823		823
Club Sport U.S.	WPOABO91CKS125001–5007		7
Carrera 4 U.S.[2]	WPOABO9CKS450001–1117	62K00001–on (M64/01)	1,117
Turbo	WPOZZZ93ZKS000001–0857	67K0051–1103 (930/66)	857
Turbo Targa	WPOZZZ93ZKS010001–0115		115

[2] See chapter 9 for information regarding the 1989 Carrera 4 models that were produced from January 1989 through July 1989. These were the first of the upgraded 911 (code 964) that used the 3.6-liter air-cooled engine.

Model	Chassis Serial No.	Engine Serial No.	Produced
Turbo Cabrio	WPOZZZ93ZKS020001–0244		244
Turbo N.A.	WPOJBO93CKS050001–0639	68K0051–1232 (930/68)	639
Turbo Targa N.A.	WPOEBO93CKS060001–0109		109
Turbo Cabrio N.A.	WPOEBO93CKS070001–0600		600

The only change from 1983 was that the 10th digit in the serial number became "K" to designate a 1989 model.

Engines
Types 930/20, 930/25, and 930/26 carried over from 1987 model year
Types 930/66 and 930/68 Turbo engines carried over from 1987 model year.

Transmissions
Types G50/00 and G50/01 carried forward from 1988 to the Carrera 3.2-liter cars
Type G50/50, basically a strengthened version of the G50/00, became the first five-speed manual transmission fitted to the Turbo models.

Exterior
Standard Colors

Color Code	Color
22C	Murano Green
60M	Linen Gray
80K	Guards Red
347	Dark Blue
548	Apricot Beige
700	Black
908	Grand Prix White

Special Order Colors

Color Code	Color
22D	Slate Gray Metallic
22E	Forest Green Metallic
37B	Baltic Blue Metallic
40L	Cognac Brown Metallic

Color Code	Color *(continued)*
55	Linen Gray Metallic
81K	Coral Metallic
81L	Velvet Red
693	Stone Gray Metallic
697	Diamond Blue Metallic
980	Silver Metallic

Interior

Leatherette (vinyl) standard:
> Cashmire Beige, Burgundy, Linen Gray, Mahogany, Blue, Black

Leather, optional:
> Cashmire Beige, Blue, Black, Velvet Red, Linen Gray, Silk Gray, Slate Gray, Caramel, Burgundy, Venetian Blue, and Mahogany

Additional no-cost options:
> Pinstripe velour:
>> Mahogany/White, Black/White, Burgundy/White, Linen Gray/White, Blue/White, Cashmire Beige/White

> Multi-color studio check:
>> Mahogany, Black, Blue, Linen Gray, Burgundy, Cashmire Beige

> "Porsche" script diagonal pattern cloth:
>> Black, Mahogany, Cashmire Beige, Linen Gray, Blue, Burgundy

Note: All of the above interiors were available on Turbo models.

Carpets:
> Silk velour:
>> Silk Gray, Mahogany, Blue, Linen Gray, Black, Slate Gray, Velvet Red, Burgundy, Cashmire Beige, Caramel, Venetian Blue

Cabriolet top:
> Black, Mahogany, Blue, Burgundy

Options

See note and listing for 1978 model year

Speedster On sale starting January 1989 through September 1989. Offered in slant-nose and Turbo Look body styles but only the Turbo Look was sold in Germany and the United States. Of 2,065 models produced, 1,894 were Turbo Look; 823 cars came to the U.S.

Chapter Nine

1989–1993, Carrera 2/4

1989: In January 1989, midway through the 1989 model year, Porsche began production of a new series of 911s, designated internally as 964, that were claimed to be "87 percent new" compared to their predecessors, which dated back to 1963. The Carrera 4 coupe was the first of the 964 lineup. It had a larger, 3.6-liter engine, but its most distinguishing characteristic was the all-wheel-drive system that was reminiscent of the 959 and its 961 race car siblings. A five-speed gearbox, based on the G50, transferred power to a front differential via a rigid torque tube that carried a central driveshaft. A transfer case split engine torque, with 31 percent directed to the front wheels and 69 percent to the rear. ABS wheel sensors were used to detect wheel spin and redirect torque as needed (up to 100 percent) from front to rear or vice versa as needed.

The 3.6-liter engine featured a dual-spark ignition with two plugs per cylinder, ceramic port liners to reduce heat transfer from the exhaust to the cylinder head, knock sensors, and hydraulic chain tensioners. It produced the same horsepower, 250 horsepower, in all markets with or without catalytic converters.

New bumpers front and rear, made of thermoplastic, were part of a more aerodynamically efficient body. The rear spoiler was raised or lowered automatically based on the vehicle's speed. A smooth undertray was used for improved aerodynamics. Front suspension was MacPherson struts with light alloy transverse arms and coil-over shocks. The rear suspension was light alloy semi-trailing arms and coil-over shocks. All-wheel ABS braking and power steering were also standard equipment.

The revised instrument panel included 13 warning lights and climate system controls borrowed from the 944. Option M573 added an automatic heating and air conditioning system.

New wheels, designated Club Sport, were of a smooth-faced, seven-spoke, slightly convex style. Size remained the same as the

A virtually all-new 911 was debuted in 1990. Porsche claimed to have replaced 87 percent of the parts used in the car. This is a 1990 Carrera 2 coupe.

previous 911 Carrera, 6Jx16 front and 8Jx16 rear. Tire size also remained the same at 205/55ZR and 225/50ZR, respectively.

1990: All models of the previous Carrera were discontinued including the Turbo. The Carrera 2 debuted as the rear-wheel-drive version of the Carrera 4. Both Carrera 2 and 4 were available in coupe, Targa, or Cabriolet body styles. The Cabriolet had a power-operated top as standard equipment.

In January 1990, the Carrera 2 could be ordered with an optional Tiptronic transmission. The computer-controlled, four-speed Tiptronic could be shifted manually or left in the fully automatic mode. Both Carrera 4 and 2 five-speed manual transmissions were fitted with a dual-mass flywheel. The Tiptronic option included an on-board computer that calculated outside temperature, fuel consumption, and speed/distance traveled.

The Carrera 2 was equipped with dual-piston rear brake calipers; while the Carrera 4 had four-piston rear calipers. Anti-roll bars in both the Carrera 2 and Carrera 4 measured 20 millimeters, front and rear. The rear anti-roll bar on Tiptronic-equipped cars was 19 millimeters. U.S. cars were equipped with dual airbags (driver and passenger side) as standard equipment.

U.S. prices: Carrera 2 coupe, $58,500; Targa, $59,900; Cabriolet, $66,800. Carrera 4 coupe, $69,500; Targa, $70,900; Cabriolet, $77,800.

Competition/Sport: Carrera Cup race cars were based on the Carrera 2 but had engines selected at the factory for identical power output, no air filter, no dual-mass flywheel, and sealed engine control units—all to ensure equal performance. Equipped with the 911 Turbo brake system, other safety features included alloy wheels designed to retain tires despite air pressure loss, and welded-in steel roll cages by Matter.

1991: The Turbo returned in September 1990, using the chassis of the Carrera 2/4 with a 3.3-liter engine fitted with a new turbocharger and larger intercooler. Transmission was the five-speed G50. The brake system employed ABS and larger discs, 322 millimeter (12.68 inches) front, and 299 millimeter (11.77 inches) rear. Wheels were 17-inch Cup Design, 7J front with 205/50ZR tires and 9J rear with 255/45ZR tires. Approved tire brands were Bridgestone, Pirelli, and Yokohama. The front anti-roll bar was 21 millimeters and the rear 22 millimeters.

Dual airbags became standard on all left-hand-drive cars beginning February 1991. The M030 Sport Suspension with stiffer shocks and springs was available for the Carrera 2.

U.S. prices: Carrera 2 coupe, $61,915; Targa, $63,445; Cabriolet, $70,690. Carrera 4 coupe, $73,440; Targa, $74,970; Cabriolet, $82,215; Turbo coupe, $95,000.

1992: ZF power steering was altered on the Carrera 2/4 to include steering stops for use of 17-inch wheels. The Carrera 2 for the United

States received alloy four-piston rear calipers from the Carrera 4 with a brake proportioning valve to prevent rear wheel lock-up.

The Carrera 2 Cabriolet could be ordered with a Turbo Look that included the suspension, brakes, 17-inch wheels, and fender flares of the Turbo but retained the Carrera 2 engine and transmission. This model was referred to as the America Roadster.

Keylock and Shiftlock were added to U.S. and Canadian versions of the Tiptronic.

Competition / Sport: The Carrera 2 RS developed as a lightweight competition version of the production Carrera 2. It was offered in the Basic version, which weighed in at 2,684 pounds devoid of interior trim and accessories like air conditioning, sunroof, alarm system, and power windows. A Touring model that weighed 2,904 pounds restored some accessories for more comfortable road use. Two other race-track-only versions were the Competition version and Carrera Cup version.

For customers in the U.S. and Canada, the RS America was offered instead of the Carrera 2 RS. It was slightly heavier than the RoW RS, weighing in at 2,954 pounds. There were 45 Carrera Cup USA cars produced for a series that never materialized.

Available by special order was the Turbo S, a lightweight Turbo model similar to the Carrera 2 RS that weighed 2,844 pounds with a 381-horsepower engine. In all, 80 of these cars were built.

1993: Type 964 model production ended in December 1993. As of the 1993 model year all Porsche engines were factory-filled with synthetic motor oil. CFC-free refrigerant was used in all air conditioning systems. All right-hand-drive models were fitted with a driver's-side airbag. Four-piston rear calipers were fitted to the worldwide production version of the Carrera 2. Keylock and Shiftlock were added to all versions of the Tiptronic.

Production of the 3.6-liter Turbo model began in January 1993. The suspension was similar to the 3.3 Turbo's but lowered by 20 millimeters and featured a front shock tower brace. Wheels were a three-piece Cup Design: 8Jx18 with 225/40ZR tires front and 10Jx18 with 265/35ZR tires rear.

The Carrera 2 Speedster was option M503 on a Cabriolet chassis. A run of 3,000 was planned but only 936 were built. A limited run of 911 "Celebration" cars was built starting in March 1993 to commemorate 30 years of 911 production.

U.S. prices: Carrera 2 coupe, $64,990; Targa, $66,600; Cabriolet, $74,190. Carrera 4 coupe, $77,050; Targa, $78,660.

Competition / Sport: About 100 RS 3.8 models were built for GT racing. These cars were distinguished by a large, adjustable biplane rear wing on a Turbo Look body. The nonturbocharged engine had a capacity of 3,746 cc and produced 300 horsepower. They were equipped with Speedline 9Jx18 front wheels with 235/40ZR Dunlop tires in front and 11Jx18 wheels with 285/35ZR tires in rear.

Dimensions	1990–94 C2
Wheelbase:	89.4 inches
Height:	51.9 inches
Width:	65 inches
Weight, 911	2,970 lbs
Weight, Turbo	3,234 lbs
Fuel tank capacity	20.0 gallons

L Program – Produced from August 1989 to July 1990

Model	Chassis Serial No.	Engine Serial No.	Produced
Carrera	WPOZZZ96ZLS400001–3957	62L00001–on (M64/01)	3,957
Carrera Targa	WPOZZZ96ZLS410001–0322		322
Carrera Cabrio	WPOZZZ96ZLS420001–0895		895
Carrera U.S.	WPOAB296CLS450001–1317		1,317
Carrera Canada	WPOAB096CLS459001–9080		80
Carrera Targa U.S.	WPOBB296CLS460001–0158		158
Carrera Targa Canada	WPOBB096CLS469001–9061		61
Carrera Cabrio U.S.	WPOCB296CLS470001–0673		673
Carrera Cabrio Canada	WPOCB096CLS479001–9061		61

Serial number code changes were as follows: The tenth digit was changed to "L" to designate the 1990 model year. The fourth digit on U.S. cars reflected the body style, A = Coupe, B = Targa, C = Cabriolet. The fifth digit on U.S. cars was "2" to indicate the inclusion of airbags. The new model designation of 964 is shown by the seventh and eighth digits, which changed to "96," and the twelfth, which became "4."

The Carrera 2 was introduced in January 1990. Carrera 4 production started in January 1989.

Engines

Type M64/01 fitted to all Carrera 4 and Carrera 2 models

Bore increased to 100-millimeter x stroke increased to 76.4-millimeter

3.6-liter, 3,600 cc

Ceramic port liners in cylinder heads for exhaust passages

Forged pistons with dished crowns

Knock sensors

Lighter crankshaft

Twin-plug ignition, two spark plugs per cylinder

Redesigned, hydraulic chain tensioners
Compression ratio of 11.3:1 for all models
12-blade cooling fan
Fuel requirement 95 RON
DME with sequential fuel injection
250 horsepower @ 6,100 rpm
228 foot-pounds torque @ 4,800 rpm
Option M 150 deleted catalytic converters and oxygen sensors
    for countries w/o unleaded fuel
Type M64/02 fitted to Tiptronic-equipped Carrera 2 models. Same
as M64/01. No Turbo models in 1990 model year

Transmissions
Type G64/00 five-speed manual fitted to all Carrera 4 models
    Split engine torque between front wheels (31percent) and rear
      wheels (69 percent)
Type G64/01 five-speed manual fitted to Swiss Carrera 4 models
    Same as G64/00 with lower fourth and fifth gear ratios for
      noise reduction
Type G50/01 four-speed Tiptronic available on Carrera 2 models
    Fully automatic or manually shifted modes
Type G50/03 five-speed manual fitted to Carrera 2

Exterior
Standard Colors

Color Code	Color
22C	Murano Green
35V	Marine Blue Metallic
60M	Linen Gray
80K	Guards Red
347	Dark Blue
548	Apricot Beige
700	Black
908	Grand Prix White

Special Order Colors

Color Code	Color
	Tahoe Blue Metallic
22L	Oak Green Metallic
35U	Venetian Blue Metallic
50	Satin Blue Metallic
52	Cassis Red Metallic
53	Granite Green Metallic
54	Lagoon Green Metallic
55	Zermatt Silver Metallic
57	Violet Blue Metallic
59	Turquoise Metallic

Dual airbags became standard equipment on all LHD Carreras, such as this Carrera 2 Targa, in April 1991.

Interior

Leatherette (vinyl) standard:
Cashmire Beige, Burgundy, Linen Gray, Mahogany, Blue, Black
Leather, optional:
Cashmire Beige, Blue, Black, Velvet Red, Linen Gray, Silk Gray, Slate Gray, Caramel, Burgundy, Venetian Blue, and Mahogany
Additional no-cost options:
Pinstripe velour:
Mahogany/White, Black/White, Burgundy/White, Linen Gray/White, Blue/White, Cashmire Beige/White
Multi-color studio check:
Mahogany, Black, Blue, Linen Gray, Burgundy, Cashmire Beige
"Porsche Script" diagonal pattern cloth:
Black, Mahogany, Cashmire Beige, Linen Gray, Blue, Burgundy
Note: All of the above interiors were available on Turbo models.
Carpets:
Silk velour:
Silk Gray, Mahogany, Blue, Linen Gray, Black, Slate Gray, Velvet Red, Burgundy, Cashmire Beige, Caramel, Venetian Blue
Cabriolet top:
Black, Mahogany, Blue, Burgundy

Options

See note and listing for 1978 model year
M659 on-board computer option debuted
Power top became standard equipment on all Cabriolets
Dual airbags on U.S. Carrera

M Program – Produced from August 1990 to July 1991

Model	Chassis Serial No.	Engine Serial No.	Produced
Carrera	WPOZZZ96ZMS400001–7840	62M00001–on (M64/01)	7,840
Carrera Targa	WPOZZZ96ZMS430001–1196		1,196
Carrera Cabrio	WPOZZZ96ZMS450001–3886		3,886
Carrera U.S.	WPOAB296CMS410001–1608		1,608
Carrera Targa U.S.	WPOBB296CMS440001–0746		746
Carrera Cabrio U.S.	WPOCB296CMS460001–2207		2,207
Turbo	WPOZZZ96ZMS470001–2298	61M00001–on (M30/69)	2,298
Turbo U.S.	WPOAA296CMS480001–0674		674
Carrera . Cup	WPOZZZ96ZMS409001–9120	62M00001–on (M64/01)	120

Serial number code changes were as follows: The 10th digit was changed to "M" to designate the 1991 model year.

Engines

Type M64/01 carried over from 1990 for all manual transmission
  Carrera 2 and 4 models
Type M64/02 carried over from 1990 for Tiptronic Carrera 2 models
Type M30/69 fitted to Turbo models
  97-millimeter bore x 74.4-millimeter stroke
  3.3-liter, 3,299 cc
  Stainless steel cylinder head gasket
  Larger intercooler than previous 3.3-liter turbo
  Larger turbocharger
  7.0:1 compression ratio
  Three-way catalytic converters
  Fuel requirement 95 RON, unleaded
  320 horsepower @ 5,750 rpm
  332 foot-pounds torque @ 4,500 rpm

Transmissions

Type G64/00 five-speed manual fitted to all Carrera 4 models as in 1990
  Split engine torque between front wheels (31 percent) and rear
    wheels (69 percent)
Type G64/01 five-speed manual fitted to Swiss Carrera 4 models as
  in 1990
  Same as G64/00 with lower fourth and fifth gear ratios for
    noise reduction

Type A50/01 four-speed Tiptronic available on Carrera 2 models as
in 1990

Fully automatic or manually shifted modes

Type G50/03 five-speed manual fitted to Carrera 2 as in 1990

Type G50/52 five-speed manual fitted to Turbo models (two-wheel
drive only)

ZF mechanical limited-slip differential standard equipment

20 percent lock-up under load; 100 percent lock-up under braking

Exterior
Standard Colors

Color Code	Color
22R	Mint Green
22S	Signal Green
80K	Guards Red
82N	Rubystone Red
388	Maritime Blue
700	Black
908	Grand Prix White

Special Order Colors

Color Code	Color
22D	Slate Gray Metallic
22L	Oak Green Metallic
37U	Cobalt Blue Metallic
37W	Midnight Blue Metallic
37X	Horizon Blue Metallic
37Z	Amazon Green Metallic
38A	Amethyst Metallic
82H	Coral Red Metallic
92E	Polar Silver Metallic
738	Black Metallic

Interior

Leatherette (vinyl) standard:

Cashmire Beige, Light Gray, Magenta, Cobalt Blue, Black,
Classic Gray

Leather, optional:

Cashmire Beige, Cobalt Blue, Black, Matador Red, Light Gray,
Classic Gray, Carrera Gray, Magenta, Sherwood Green

Additional no-cost options:

Multi-color studio check:

Magenta, Black, Cobalt Blue, Classic Gray, Light Gray,
Cashmire Beige

"Porsche Script" diagonal pattern cloth:

Black, Magenta, Cashmire Beige, Light Gray, Classic Gray,
Cobalt Blue

Note: All of the above interiors were available on Turbo models.
Carpets:
Silk velour:
Classic Gray, Magenta, Cobalt Blue, Light Gray, Black,
Carrera Gray, Matador Red, Cashmire Beige, Sherwood Green
Cabriolet top:
Black, Mahogany, Blue, Burgundy

Options

See note and listing for 1978 model year
Beginning April 1991 dual airbags became standard on all left-hand-drive production cars.

N Program – Produced from August 1991 to July 1992

Model	Chassis Serial No.	Engine Serial No.	Produced
Carrera	WPOZZZ96ZNS400001–4844	62N00001–on (M64/01)	4,844
Carrera Targa	WPOZZZ96ZNS430001–0597		597
Carrera Cabrio	WPOZZZ96ZNS450001–2885		2,885
Carrera U.S.	WPOAB296CNS420001–0715		715
Carrera Targa U.S.	WPOBB296CNS440001–0211		211
Carrera Cabrio U.S.	WPOCB296CNS460001–0992		992
Turbo	WPOZZZ96ZNS470001–0836	61N00001–on (M30/69)	836
Turbo U.S.	WPOAA296CNS480001–0309		309
Carrera RS	WPOZZZ96ZNS490001–2500	62N80001–on (M64/03)	1992
Carrera RS Competition	WPOZZZ96ZSN499001-9300	62N80001-on	290
Carrera Cup	WPOZZZ96ZNS498001-8150	62N80001-on	112
Carrera RS America	WPOAB296CPS418001–8298	62N00001–on (M64/01)	298

Serial number code changes were as follows: The 10th digit was changed to "N" to designate the 1992 model year.

Engines

Type M64/01 carried over from 1991 for all manual transmission
Carrera 2 and 4 models including U.S. 911 RS America
and Carrera Cup cars
Type M64/02 carried over from 1991 for Tiptronic Carrera 2 models

Type M30/69 carried over from 1991 for Turbo models

Type M30/69SL fitted to special order run of Turbo S models. Same as M30/69 except:

Fuel requirement 98 RON

Remapped DME

381 horsepower @ 6,000 rpm

362 foot-pounds torque @ 4,800 rpm

Type M64/03 fitted to Carrera RS except for U.S. RS America

Matched pistons and cylinders

Lightweight sport flywheel

Fuel requirement 98 RON, unleaded

260 horsepower @ 6,100 rpm

240 foot-pounds torque @ 5,000 rpm

Transmissions

Turbo pedal cluster with spring-assisted clutch pedal was fitted to all normally aspirated cars

Type G64/00 five-speed manual fitted to all Carrera 4 models

Type G64/01 five-speed manual fitted to Swiss Carrera 4 models as in 1990

Same as G64/00 with lower fourth and fifth gear ratios for noise reduction

Type A50/02 four-speed Tiptronic available on RoW Carrera 2 models

Type A50/03 four-speed Tiptronic available for U.S. and Canada Carrera 2 models. Improvements made to A50/03:

Shiftlock added—brake must be applied to move shift lever out of "Park" position

The 1993 Turbo received a 3.6-liter, 360-horsepower engine.

A lightweight sport version of the Carrera 2 came to the U.S. as the 1993 RS America.

Transmissions *(continued)*

Keylock added—ignition key can only be removed while shift
     lever is in "Park" position
     Final drive ratio of 9:32
Type G50/03 five-speed manual fitted to Carrera 2
Type G50/52 five-speed manual fitted to Turbo models (including
     Turbo S)
     ZF mechanical limited-slip differential standard equipment
     (20 percent lock-up under load; 100 percent lockup under braking)
Type G50/10 five-speed manual transmission fitted to Carrera RS models
     Taller first and second gears than G50/03
     Limited-slip differential from Turbo is standard equipment
     Steel synchronizer rings, altered shift sleeves
     "Short shifter" fitted for sportier feel

Exterior
Standard Colors

Color Code	Color
N4	Mint Green
M1	Signal Green
G1	Guards Red
G4	Rubystone Red
F2	Maritime Blue
A1	Black
P5	Grand Prix White

Special Order Colors

Color Code	Color
Q9	Slate Gray Metallic
N9	Oak Green Metallic
F6	Cobalt Blue Metallic
F8	Midnight Blue Metallic
Z8	Blue Metallic
N7	Amazon Green Metallic

The last year for the Type 964 Carrera 2 Cabriolet was 1994. It was replaced in the spring of 1994 by the new 993 Cabriolet.

Color Code	**Color** *(continued)*
F9	Amethyst Metallic
G7	Coral Red Metallic
A8	Polar Silver Metallic
50	Satin Blue Metallic
52	Cassis Red Metallic
53	Granite Green Metallic
54	Lagoon Green Metallic
55	Zermatt Silver Metallic
56	Marine Blue Metallic
57	Violet Blue Metallic
59	Turquoise Metallic

Turbo Look special order colors:

    Raspberry Red Metallic w/Red interior

    Wimbledon Green Metallic w/ Green interior

    Lavender Blue Metallic w/Gray interior

Interior

Leatherette (vinyl) standard:

    Cashmire Beige, Light Gray, Magenta, Cobalt Blue, Black, Classic Gray

Leather, optional:

    Cashmire Beige, Cobalt Blue, Black, Matador Red, Light Gray, Classic Gray, Carrera Gray, Magenta, Sherwood Green

Additional no-cost options:

    Multi-color studio check:

        Blue, Cobalt Blue, Classic Gray, Light Gray, Cashmire Beige

    "Porsche" script diagonal pattern cloth:

        Black, Magenta, Cashmire Beige, Light Gray, Classic Gray, Cobalt Blue

Note: All of the above interiors were available on Turbo models.
Carpets:

Silk velour:

Classic Gray, Magenta, Cobalt Blue, Light Gray, Black,
Carrera Gray, Matador Red, Cashmire Beige, Sherwood
Green

Cabriolet top:

Black, Magenta, Dark Blue, Cobalt Blue

Options

See note and listing for 1978 model year

Carrera 2 RS   Powered by 260-horsepower Type M64/03 engine.
Close ratio G50 transmission with limited-slip differential.
Weight (Sport [standard] version) was 2,712 pounds. Deleted to
save weight were sunroof, electric mirrors, power seats, central
locking, alarm, power windows, and associated wiring harness-
es. No rear seats, sound insulation, or undercoating. Thinner
side glass, 3-millimeter versus 4.7-millimeter thick. Safety harness instead of airbags. Nonassisted steering. Equipped with
Recaro sport seats (manual), lightweight rear bumper, aluminum trunk lid, 92-liter fuel tank, stiffer springs and shocks
(40 millimeter lower ride height), 24-millimeter front anti-roll
bar, 18-millimeter rear anti-roll bar, limited slip differential,
Turbo front brakes, 322-millimeter disc, Carrera Cup 299-
millimeter disc in rear, and Cup Design alloy wheels: 7.5Jx17
front, 9Jx17 rear. Tires: 205/50ZR17 and 255/40ZR17. Not sold
in the United States. Cost: about $97,000 (U.S.). Total produc-
tion was 2282 cars including 1916 Basic models (72 RHD), 76
Touring versions (11RHD), and 290 competition cars.

M001   *Carrera Cup* version   120 cars made for the Carrera Cup
racing series

M002   *Touring* version   Weighed 2,866 pounds. Equipped with
stereo/cassette, central locking, sound insulation, undercoating, power windows, power sport seats, and Carrera 2 door
panels and interior trim. It also had the stock wiring harness
and available options like power sunroof, heated seats, headlamp washers, and climate control.

M003   *GroupN GTI*   FIA racing version of Carrera Cup cars

M504   *RS America*   Option M504   Lighter weight, sport-ori-
ented version of Carrera 2 sold only in the United States and
Canada. Powered by the standard Type M64/01 engine. Weight:
2,955 pounds. Deleted to save weight were air conditioning,
power steering, power sunroof, sound insulation, and rear
seats. A whale tail rear spoiler replaced the stock moveable
unit. Seats were black corduroy fabric. Options included air
conditioning, sunroof, stereo, and limited-slip differential.
Equipped with M030 sports suspension, 22-millimeter front

anti-roll bars, 20-millimeter rear anti-roll bars, Cup Design alloy wheels: 7Jx17 front, 8Jx17 rear. Tires: 205/50ZR17 and 255/40ZR17. Cost: $53,900

America Roadster Turbo Look Cabriolet with normally aspirated 3.6-liter engine. Available with manual or Tiptronic transmission, Turbo brakes, full leather interior, power top, and moveable rear spoiler instead of Turbo tail. Anti-roll bars were 21 millimeters front, 22 millimeters rear except on Tiptronic-equipped cars, which had 21-millimeter rear bars. A total of 250 of these were produced.

Turbo S Special order lightweight Turbo model similar to Carrera RS. Weight: 2,844 pounds, approximately 419 pounds less than a stock Turbo. Powered my Type M30/69SL modified Turbo engine. Recaro sport seats, cloth door pulls, wind-up windows, no rear seats, no radio, thinner rear and side window glass, simplified wiring harness, composite doors, engine lid, and trunk lid. Whale-tail rear wing, air scoops in rear fenders, and air intakes replaced driving lights in the front spoiler. Stiffer suspension. Speedline three-piece wheels 8Jx18 front, 10Jx18 rear. Tires: Pirelli P Zero 235/40ZR and 265/35ZR. Red brake calipers. Total production: 80 cars

Carrera Cup USA Forty-five cars were imported to the United States for a Carrera Cup series that never materialized. The cars were the Carrera RS Basic model as sold in Europe except for the addition of safety door beams, U.S. bumpers, fog lights, power windows, central locking, airbags, and standard seats. Wheels were the same as those on the RS America. Twenty-five of these cars were converted by Andial to full Carrera Cup specifications but were then reconverted after the series was canceled. All of the cars were Grand Prix White with black

The RS America was designed to be a lighter-weight alternative for club racing and time trials in the United Sates and Canada.

interiors except for one that was Guards Red. The cars carry a special Carrera Cup USA dash plaque bearing their VIN. The 25 cars that were originally coverted by Andial also bear separate serial numbers from 92 01 to 92 25 to further distinguish them. The VINs for these cars are not consecutive and fall in the range for U.S./Canada Carrera 2 coupes for the year 1992. The first car is WPOAB296CNS420392 and the last car is WPO-AB296CN420602. The red car's serial number ends in 20509.

P Program – Produced from August 1992 to July 1993

Model	Chassis Serial No.	Engine Serial No.	Produced
Carrera	WPOZZZ96ZPS400001–3249	62P00001–on (M64/01)	3,249
Carrera Targa	WPOZZZ96ZPS430001–0419		419
Carrera Cabrio	WPOZZZ96ZPS450001–1414		1,414
Carrera U.S./Canada	WPOAB296CPS420001–0520		520
Carrera Targa U.S./Canada	WPOBB296CPS440001–0137		137
Carrera Cabrio U.S./Canada	WPOCB296CPS460001–0600		600
Turbo (begins Jan. 1993)	WPOZZZ96ZPS470001–0650	61P00001–on (M64/50)	650
Carrera RS America	WPOAB296CPS419001–9450	62P00001–on (M64/01)	450
Carrera RS 3.8	WPOZZZ96ZPS497001–7129	62P85001–on (M64/04)	992

Serial number code changes were as follows: The 10th digit changed to "P" to designate the 1993 model year.

Note: U.S./Canada cars made after May 1993 were designated as "R" program cars, making them 1994 models.

Engines

Type M64/01 carried over from 1992 for all manual transmission
   Carrera 2 and 4 models including U.S. 911 RS America
Type M64/02 carried over from 1992 for Tiptronic Carrera 2 models
Type M64/04 fitted to Carrera RS 3.8
   3.8-liter, 3,746 cc
   Nonturbocharged
   Compression ratio 11.0:1
   Motronic 2.1 engine management system
   300 horsepower @ 6,500 rpm
   266 foot-pounds torque @ 5,250 rpm

Type M64/50 Turbo fitted to Turbo models as of January 1993
  3.6-liter, 3,600 cc
  Compression ratio is 7.5:1
  Single-plug cylinder heads
  360 horsepower @ 5,500 rpm
  383 foot-pounds torque @ 4,200 rpm

Racing Engines
Type M64/04 fitted to Carrera RSR 3.8
  Bosch Motronic 2.1 engine management system
  Compression ratio 11.3:1
  350 horsepower @ 6,900 rpm
  284 foot-pounds torque @ 5,000 rpm

Transmissions
Type G64/00 five-speed manual fitted to all Carrera 4 models
Type A50/02 four-speed Tiptronic available on RoW Carrera 2 models
  Shiftlock and Keylock added as on 1992 U.S. Tiptronic
Type A50/03 four-speed Tiptronic available for U.S. and Canada
  Carrera 2 models
Type G50/03 five-speed manual fitted to Carrera 2
Type G50/52 five-speed manual fitted to Turbo models
  ZF mechanical limited-slip differential standard equipment
  (20 percent lock-up under load; 100 percent lock-up under
  braking)
Type G50/10 five-speed manual transmission fitted to Carrera RS
  3.8 models
  Taller first and second gears than G50/03
  Limited-slip differential from Turbo is standard equipment
  Steel synchronizer rings, altered shift sleeves
  "Short shifter" fitted for sportier feel

*The Turbo Look option package, as seen on this 1994 Carrera 4,
included the wide body, larger wheels, brakes, and suspension used
on the Turbo model.*

Exterior
Standard Colors

Color Code	Color
N4	Mint Green
M1	Signal Green
G1	Guards Red
F2	Maritime Blue
A1	Black
P5	Grand Prix White

Special Order Colors

Color Code	Color
Q9	Slate Gray Metallic
A7	Raspberry Red Metallic
B5	Wimbledon Green Metallic
N9	Oak Green Metallic
F6	Cobalt Blue Metallic
F8	Midnight Blue Metallic
Z8	Black Metallic
N7	Amazon Green Metallic
F9	Amethyst Metallic
X4	Speed Yellow
A8	Polar Silver Metallic
50	Satin Blue Metallic
52	Cassis Red Metallic
53	Granite Green Metallic
54	Lagoon Green Metallic
55	Zermatt Silver Metallic
56	Marine Blue Metallic
57	Violet Blue Metallic
59	Turquoise Metallic

Interior
Leatherette (vinyl) standard:
    Cashmire Beige, Light Gray, Magenta, Cobalt Blue, Black, or
    Classic Gray
Leather, optional:
    Cashmire Beige, Cobalt Blue, Black, Matador Red, Light Gray,
    Classic Gray, Carrera Gray, Magenta, or Sherwood Green
Additional no-cost options:
    Multi-color studio check:
        Blue, Cobalt Blue, Classic Gray, Light Gray, or Cashmire
        Beige

"Porsche" script diagonal pattern cloth:
> Black, Magenta, Cashmire Beige, Light Gray, Classic Gray, or Cobalt Blue

Note: All of the above interiors were available on Turbo models.

Carpets:

Silk velour:
> Classic Gray, Magenta, Cobalt Blue, Light Gray, Black, Carrera Gray, Matador Red, Cashmire Beige, or Sherwood Green

Cabriolet top:
> Black, Magenta, Dark Blue, Cobalt Blue, or Classic Gray

The Turbo was available as a 1994 model before disappearing for a year when the 993 body style came out.

Options

See note and listing for 1978 model year

Driver's-side airbag standard for all markets

All Porsche engines factory filled with Shell synthetic motor oil, SAE 5W-40

CFC-free refrigerant used in all air conditioning units

911 Celebration or "30th Anniversary Edition" Built from March 1993 to celebrate 30 years of 911 production. Carrera 4 with Turbo Look body but standard brakes and running gear. Commemorative badges on rear package shelf and script style "911" badge with "30 Jahre" inscribed on it. Exterior was Violet Metallic with full leather interior in Rubicon Gray. Production limited to 911 cars.

Carrera RS 3.8 Turbo-bodied version of Carrera RS with aluminum doors, front and rear spoilers, larger brakes, and 18-inch wheels.

Chapter Ten

1994–1998, 993 Carrera

1994: New 911 Carrera debuted in coupe body style only. The Cabriolet followed in March 1994. U.S. cars were introduced in April 1994 with the majority sold as 1995 models under option code 718. Type 964 production ended in December 1993. The 993 production began in January 1994.

The 993 had almost no parts carried over from the 964 except the roof and trunk lid. Lighter pistons and connecting rods with an upgraded engine management system raised the power of the 3.6-liter engine to 272 horsepower. Hydraulic valve lifters were also part of the engine improvements.

The rear suspension was changed from the use of semi-trailing arms to a multi-link arrangement called LSA (Lightweight, Stable, Agile). Larger ventilated and cross-drilled brake rotors were fitted up front with four-piston calipers front and rear. The front discs measured 304-millimeters (12.0 inches) and the ventilated and cross-drilled rear discs remained at 299-millimeters (11.8 inches). Cup Design 93 wheels were standard. Their spokes were designed to draw off hot air from the brakes while at speed. Front wheels were 7Jx16 with 205/55ZR tires and the rear wheels were 9Jx16 with 245/45ZR tires. A new six-speed manual transmission was fitted to the 993.

A new feature was the Porsche Electronic Immobilizer alarm system that acted upon the DME to disable the engine.

1995: A redesigned all-wheel-drive system was the main feature of the new 993 Carrera 4. The new system used a viscous coupling and central shaft to transmit power to the front wheels and weighed about half as much (111 pounds) as the computer-controlled system of the 964. ABD, Automatic Brake Differential, traction control was standard on the Carrera 4.

The Tiptronic S debuted with fingertip gear change switches on the steering wheel.

The 993 Turbo was introduced featuring two turbochargers, four-wheel drive, and six-speed transmission. Wheels were a new lightweight design called Technologie-Rad with pressure-cast hollow spokes. The 18-inch wheels were 8J in front with 225/40ZR tires and 10J at the rear with 285/30ZR tires. Brake discs were 322-millimeters (12.7 inches) all around. The 3.6-liter Turbo was priced at $99,000 in the United States.

Competition / Sport: The 993 RS debuted with a 3.8-liter engine equipped with the Varioram intake system and the new six-speed manual transmission. Porsche made available for racing the turbocharged GT2.

1996: Varioram became standard on the 993 3.6-liter engine. A new Targa debuted with a sliding glass roof panel. Carrera 4S introduced the concept of combining four-wheel drive with the Turbo's chassis and wider body minus the rear wing.

U.S. prices: 993 Carrera 2 coupe, $63,750; Targa, $70,750; Cabriolet, $73,000. 993 Carrera 4 coupe, $69,100; Cabriolet, $78,350; Carrera 4S, $73,000.

1997: The Carrera S was introduced as a two-wheel-drive version of the Carrera 4S. The Turbo S limited edition combined a custom leather interior with an exterior featuring a biplane whale-tail spoiler and air scoops in the rear fenders plus a 424-horsepower engine. U.S. price of a Turbo coupe, $105,000; Turbo S coupe, $150,000.

1998: Production of four-wheel-drive and Turbo 993 models continued until July 1998.

Dimensions	**1995–1998 993**
Wheelbase:	89.4 inches
Height:	51.8 inches
Width:	68.3 inches
Weight, 993 C2	3,014 lbs
Turbo	3,465 lbs
Fuel tank capacity	19.4 gallons

R Program – Produced from August 1993 to July 1994. Type 964 production ends December 1993. Type 993 begins January 1994.

Model (964)	Chassis Serial No.	Engine Serial No.	Produced
Carrera	WPOZZZ96ZRS400001–0505	62R00001–on (M64/01)	505
Carrera Cabrio	WPOZZZ96ZRS450001–0315		315
Carrera U.S./Canada	WPOAB296CRS420001–0456		456
Carrera Cabrio U.S./Canada	WPOCB296CRS460001–0283		283
RS America U.S./Canada	WPOAB296CRS419001–9144		144
Speedster	WPOZZZ96ZRS455001–5581		581
Speedster U.S.	WPOCB296CRS465001–5469		469
Turbo	WPOZZZ96ZRS470001–0471	61R00001–on (M64/05)	471
Turbo U.S./Canada	WPOAC296CRS480001–0466		466

Model (993)	Chassis Serial No.	Engine Serial No.	Produced
Carrera	WPOZZZ99ZRS310001–6412	63R00001–on (M64/07)	6,412
Carrera Cabriolet	WPOZZZ99ZRS330001–5850		5,850

Model (993)	Chassis Serial No.	Engine Serial No.	Produced
Carrera U.S./Canada	WPOAA299CRS320001–1453	64R00001–on (M64/70)	1,453
Carrera Cabrio U.S./Canada	WPOCA299CRS340001–1224		1,224
Carerra Cup	WPOZZZ99ZRS398001–8100	63R80001-on	100

Serial number code changes were as follows: The tenth digit changed to "R" to designate the 1994 model year. The new model designation of 993 is shown by the seventh and eighth digits, which changed to "99," and the twelfth, which became "3."

The 993 Carrera coupe debuted in 1995. Only the roof and deck lid carried over from the previous 911 when the 993 was released as a 1995 model.

Engines

964 Model 911s

Type M64/01 was carried over from 1993 for all manual transmis sion Carrera 2 and 4 models including U.S. 911 RS America and Speedster

Type M64/02 was carried over from 1993 for Tiptronic Carrera 2 models including Speedster

Type M64/50 Turbo was carried over from 1993 for Turbo 3.6 mod els through the end of their production in January 1994

993 Model 911s

Type M64/05 engine fitted to RoW 993 models
  3.6-liter, 3,600 cc
  Bosch Motronic 2.10 engine management system

Lighter pistons and connecting rods
Torsionally stiffer crankshaft
Hydraulic valve lifter adjustment
Pressure-cast aluminum cylinders w/NikaSil coating
Dual exit exhaust system
272 horsepower @ 6,100 rpm
243 foot-pounds torque @ 5,000 rpm
Designated Type M64/06 with Tiptronic
Type M64/07 fitted to U.S. 993 models
Same as Type M64/05 except for emissions fine-tuning
Designated Type M64/08 with Tiptronic

Racing Engines
Type M64/70 fitted to 993 Carrera Cup cars
Compression ratio 11.5:1
310 horsepower @ 6,200 rpm
273 foot-pounds torque @ 5,500 rpm

Transmissions
964 Model 911s
Type G64/00 five-speed manual fitted to all Carrera 4 models
Type A50/02 four-speed Tiptronic available on RoW Carrera 2 models
Type A50/03 four-speed Tiptronic available for U.S. and Canada
    Carrera 2 models
Type G50/03 five-speed manual fitted to Carrera 2
Type G50/52 five-speed manual fitted to Turbo models
    ZF mechanical limited-slip differential standard equipment
    (20 percent lock-up under load; 100 percent lock-up under braking)
993 Model 911s
Type G50/20 six-speed manual transmission for U.S. 993 models
Type G50/21 six-speed manual for RoW 993 models
Type A50/04 four-speed Tiptronic for RoW 993 models
Type A50/05 four-speed Tiptronic for U.S. 993 models
Type G50/30 six-speed manual fitted to Carrera Cup cars

The 1996 Carrera 4 coupe had a 285-horsepower engine.

Exterior
Standard Colors

Color Code	Color
X4	Speed Yellow
S8	Riviera Blue
G1	Guards Red
T3	Amaranth Violet
A1	Black
P5	Grand Prix White

Special Order Colors

Color Code	Color
Q9	Slate Gray Metallic
A8	Polar Silver Metallic
Z8	Black Metallic
F8	Midnight Blue Metallic
D3	Iris Blue Metallic
K6	Aventura Green Metallic
To sample	Solid or Metallic colors

Interior
Leatherette (vinyl) standard:
 Chestnut Brown, Midnight Blue, Black, or Classic Gray
Leatherette, two-tone (two-tone has second color covering dash, knee pad, roof liner, window pillars, sun visors, window sills, top of rear wall, and steering wheel):
 Midnight Blue/Marble Gray, or Black/Marble Gray
Leather, optional:
 Chestnut Brown, Midnight Blue, Black, or Classic Gray
Special order:
 Flamenco Red, Cedar Green, Provence Blue/Midnight Blue, or Provence Blue/Black
Custom leather available to sample.
Carpets:
 Classic Gray, Midnight Blue, Marble Gray, Black, Cashmire Beige, or Chestnut Brown
Cabriolet top:
 Black, Chestnut Brown, Dark Blue, Marble Gray, or Classic Gray

Options

MP08	Active limited-slip differential
MP14	Heated seats
MP15	Full power seats, left & right
MP31	Sport suspension, two 17-inch wheels
M058	Bumpers with impact absorbers
M224	Active brake differential

M333	Blaupunkt Paris RCR42 radio/cassette
M334	Blaupunkt Bremen RCM42 radio/cassette
M383	Sport seat, left
M387	Sport seat, right
M398	17-inch Cup Design wheels
M425	Rear wiper (coupe only)
M437	Full power seat, left only
M438	Full power seat, right only
M454	Cruise control
M490	Radio loudspeaker system
M498	Delete external model designation
M545	92-liter fuel tank
M551	Wind deflector, Cabriolet
M567	Graduated tint windshield
M573	Automatic air conditioning
M586	Lumbar support in seat, left
M513	Lumbar support in seat, right
M613	Porsche telephone, Motorola D-Netz (Germany only)
M650	Power sunroof
M659	On-board computer, standard w/Tiptronic
M692	CD changer (only w/M334 or M490)
M693	Blaupunkt London RMD42 radio/CD player

S Program – Produced from August 1994 to July 1995

Model (993)	Chassis Serial No.	Engine Serial No.	Produced
Carrera	WPOZZZ99ZSS310001–7018	63S00001–on (M64/05)	7,018
Carrera Cabriolet	WPOZZZ99ZSS330001–2878		2,878
Carrera U.S./Canada	WPOAA299CSS320001–4139	64S00001–on (M64/07)	4,139
Carrera Cabrio U.S./Canada	WPOCA299CSS340001–3718		3,718
Carrera RS	WPOZZZ99ZSS390001–0274	63S85001–on (M64/20)	274
Carerra Cup	WPOZZZ99ZSS398001–8110	63S80001–on (M64/70)	110
Turbo	WPOZZZ99ZSS370001–0078	61T00001–on (M64/60)	78

Serial number code changes were as follows: The 10th digit changed to "S" to designate the 1995 model year.

Engines

Type M64/05 engine fitted to RoW 993 models

Type M64/06 engine fitted to RoW 993 models with Tiptronic

Type M64/07 fitted to U.S. 993 models

Type M64/08 fitted to U.S. 993 models with Tiptronic
Type M64/20 fitted to Carrera RS
    Bore increased to 102-millimeter x 76.4-millimeter stroke
    3.8-liter, 3,746 cc
    Varioram variable length intake system
    300 horsepower @ 6,500 rpm
    262 foot-pounds torque @ 5,400 rpm
    A 285 horsepower @ 6,000 rpm version of this engine was an
        option for production 993s, designated Type M64/05S with
        manual transmission and Type M64/06S when coupled
        with Tiptronic
Type M64/60 Turbo motor
    3.6-liter, 3,600 cc
    Twin KKK K16 turbochargers/two intercoolers
    Bosch M5.2 engine management system
    OBD2 diagnostic system
    Compression ratio of 8.0:1
    Minimum fuel requirement, 95 RON unleaded
    Hydraulic valve adjustment
    Single-plug cylinder heads
    408 horsepower @ 5,750 rpm
    398 foot-pounds torque @ 4,500 rpm

Racing Engines
Type M64/70 fitted to 993 Carrera Cup cars
    Compression ratio 11.5:1
    310 horsepower @ 6,200 rpm
    273 foot-pounds torque @ 5,500 rpm

Transmissions
Type G50/20 six-speed manual transmission for U.S. 993 models
Type G50/21 six-speed manual for RoW 993 models
Type A50/04 four-speed Tiptronic for RoW 993 models
    Referred to as Tiptronic S because steering wheel shift but
        tons were added
Type A50/05 four-speed Tiptronic for U.S. 993 models
    Referred to as Tiptronic S because steering wheel shift but
        tons were added
Type G64/51 six-speed manual fitted to Turbo models
    Four-wheel drive with maximum power split, rear/front, 80/20
    Limited-slip differential standard
    ABD (Automatic Brake Differential) traction system standard
Type G50/30 six-speed manual fitted to Carrera Cup cars
Type G50/31 six-speed manual fitted to Carrera RS

Exterior
Standard Colors

Color Code	Color
X4	Speed Yellow
S8	Riviera Blue
G1	Guards Red
T3	Amaranth Violet
A1	Black
P5	Grand Prix White

Special Order Colors

Color Code	Color
Q9	Slate Gray Metallic
A8	Polar Silver Metallic
Z8	Black Metallic
F8	Midnight Blue Metallic
D3	Iris Blue Metallic
K6	Aventura Green Metallic
To sample	Solid or Metallic colors

Interior
Leatherette (vinyl) standard:
    Chestnut Brown, Midnight Blue, Black, Classic Gray, Cedar
    Green, Marble Gray, or Cashmire Beige
Leatherette, two-tone (two-tone has second color covering dash, knee
pad, roof liner, window pillars, sun visors, window sills, top of rear
wall, and steering wheel):
    Midnight Blue/Marble Gray, or Black/Marble Gray,
Leather, smooth or "soft, ruffled" optional:
    Chestnut Brown, Midnight Blue, Black, Classic Gray, Marble
    Gray, Cedar Green, or Cashmire Beige
Special order:
    Flamenco Red, Cedar Green, Provence Blue/Midnight Blue, or
    Provence Blue/Black
Custom leather available to sample.
"Porsche" cloth:
    Chestnut Brown, Midnight Blue, Black, Classic Gray, Cedar
    Green, Marble Gray, or Cashmire Beige
Carpets:
    Classic Gray, Midnight Blue, Marble Gray, Black, Cashmire
    Beige, or Chestnut Brown
Special order:
    Flamenco Red, Cedar Green, Provence Blue, or Rubicon Gray
Cabriolet top:
    Black, Chestnut Brown, Dark Blue, Marble Gray, or Classic Gray

The Turbo for 1995–1996 had 408 horsepower.

Options

MP08	Active Limited-slip differential
MP14	Heated seats
MP15	Full power seats, left & right
MP31	Sport suspension, two 17-inch wheels
M058	Bumpers with impact absorbers
M224	Active brake differential
M333	Blaupunkt Paris RCR42 radio/cassette
M334	Blaupunkt Bremen RCM42 radio/cassette
M383	Sport seat, left
M387	Sport seat, right
M398	17-inch Cup Design wheels
M425	Rear wiper (coupe only)
M437	Full power seat, left only
M438	Full power seat, right only
M454	Cruise control
M490	Radio loudspeaker system
M498	Delete external model designation
M545	92-liter fuel tank
M551	Wind deflector, Cabriolet
M567	Graduated tint windshield
M573	Automatic air conditioning
M586	Lumbar support in seat, left
M513	Lumbar support in seat, right
M613	Porsche telephone, Motorola D-Netz (Germany only)
M650	Power sunroof
M659	On-board computer, standard w/Tiptronic
M692	CD changer (only w/M334 or M490)
M693	Blaupunkt London RMD42 radio/CD player

Carrera RS   Powered by Type M64/20 3.8-liter engine with six-speed manual transmission. Weight: 2,820 pounds. Deleted power windows, power mirrors, central locking, headlamp washers, intermittent wipers, radio speakers, power seats, rear window defroster, airbags, and sound insulation. Equipped with simplified interior lighting, thinner window glass, aluminum trunk lid, and Recaro sport seats. Strut-tower cross brace, ball-joint front shock mounts, adjustable anti-roll bars, ABD and a limited-slip differential, and whale-tail rear spoiler. Wheels: 8Jx18 front, 10Jx18 rear. Tires: 225/40ZR18 front, 265/35ZR18 rear.

T Program – Produced from August 1995 to July 1996

Model (993)	Chassis Serial No.	Engine Serial No.	Produced
Carrera	WPOZZZ99ZTS310001–6762	63T00001–on (M64/21)	6,762
Carrera Targa	WPOZZZ99ZTS380001–1980		1,980
Carrera Cabriolet	WPOZZZ99ZTS330001–2066		2,066
Carrera U.S./Canada	WPOAA299CTS320001–3671	64T00001–on (M64/23)	3,671
Carrera Targa U.S./Canada	WPOBA299CTS385001–5462		462
Carrera Cabrio U.S./Canada	WPOCA299CTS340001–2152		2,152
Turbo	WPOZZZ99ZTS370001–2484	61T00001–on (M64/60)	2,484
Turbo U.S./Canada	WPOAA299CTS375001–6357		1,357
GT2	WPOZZZ99ZTS392001–2202		202

Serial number code changes were as follows: The 10th digit changed to "T" to designate the 1996 model year.

Engines

Type M64/21 engine fitted to RoW 993 models

    OBD2 Diagnostic system

    Varioram intake system added to Type M64/05

    285 horsepower @ 6,100 rpm

    251 foot-pounds torque @ 5,250 rpm

    Designated Type M64/22 engine fitted to RoW 993 models with Tiptronic

Type M64/23 fitted to U.S. 993 models

    U.S. version of Type M64/21

    Designated Type M64/24 fitted to U.S. 993 models with Tiptronic

Type M64/21S optional on manual transmission 993 models.

Similar to Type M64/20 fitted to 1995 Carrera RS

    3.8-liter, 3,746 cc

    Varioram variable length intake system

    300 horsepower @ 6,500 rpm

Engines *(continued)*
Designated Type M64/22S for Tiptronic-equipped 993 models
Type M64/60 fitted to all Turbo models

Racing Engines
Type M64/60R fitted to GT2
Racing version of M64/60 Turbo motor
Compression ratio 8.0:1
430 horsepower @ 5,750 rpm (road legal); racing version
480 horsepower
273 foot-pounds torque @ 5,500 rpm

Transmissions
Type G50/20 six-speed manual transmission for U.S. 993 models
Type G50/21 six-speed manual for RoW 993 models
Type A50/04 four-speed Tiptronic for RoW 993 models
Called Tiptronic S because steering wheel shift buttons were
added
Type A50/05 four-speed Tiptronic for U.S. 993 models
Called Tiptronic S because steering wheel shift buttons were
added
Type G64/51 six-speed manual fitted to Turbo models
Four-wheel drive with maximum power split, rear/front, 80/20
Limited-slip differential standard
ABD traction system standard
Type G50/32 six-speed manual fitted to GT2

Exterior
Standard Colors

Color Code	Color
X4	Speed Yellow
G1	Guards Red
J1	Blue Turquoise
A1	Black
P5	Grand Prix White

Special Order Colors

Color Code	Color
A8	Polar Silver Metallic
Z8	Black Metallic
F8	Midnight Blue Metallic
H8	Arena Red Metallic
D3	Iris Blue Metallic
K1	Turquoise Metallic
K6	Aventura Green Metallic
To sample	Solid or Metallic colors

The first year for the sliding-glass-roof Targa model was 1996.

Interior

Leatherette (vinyl) standard:
    Chestnut Brown, Midnight Blue, Black, Classic Gray, Cedar
    Green, Marble Gray, or Cashmire Beige

Two-tone (two-tone has second color covering dash, knee pad, roof
liner, window pillars, sun visors, window sills, top of rear wall, and
steering wheel):
    Midnight Blue/Marble Gray, or Black/Marble Gray,

Leather, smooth or "soft, ruffled" optional:
    Chestnut Brown, Midnight Blue, Black, Classic Gray, or
    Cashmire Beige

Special order:
    Rubicon Gray, Flamenco Red, Cedar Green, Provence Blue/
    Midnight Blue, or Provence Blue/Black

Custom leather available to sample.

"Porsche" cloth:
    Chestnut Brown, Midnight Blue, Black, Classic Gray, Cedar
    Green, Marble Gray, or Cashmire Beige

Carpets:
    Classic Gray, Midnight Blue, Marble Gray, Black, Cashmire
    Beige, or Chestnut Brown

Special order:
    Flamenco Red, Cedar Green, Provence Blue, or Rubicon Gray

Cabriolet top:
    Black, Chestnut Brown, Dark Blue, Marble Gray, or Classic Gray

Options

MP08	Active Limited-slip differential
MP14	Heated seats
MP15	Full power seats, left & right
MP31	Sport suspension, two 17-inch wheels

M058	Bumpers with impact absorbers
M224	Active brake differential
M333	Blaupunkt Paris RCR42 radio/cassette
M334	Blaupunkt Bremen RCM42 radio/cassette
M383	Sport seat, left
M387	Sport seat, right
M398	17-inch Cup Design wheels
M425	Rear wiper (coupe only)
M437	Full power seat, left only
M438	Full power seat, right only
M454	Cruise control
M490	Radio loudspeaker system
M498	Delete external model designation
M545	92-liter fuel tank
M551	Wind deflector, Cabriolet
M567	Graduated tint windshield
M573	Automatic air conditioning
M586	Lumbar support in seat, left
M513	Lumbar support in seat, right
M613	Porsche telephone, Motorola D-Netz (Germany only)
M650	Power sunroof
M659	On-board computer, standard w/Tiptronic
M692	CD changer (only w/M334 or M490)
M693	Blaupunkt London RMD42 radio/CD player

The 1996 Carrera 4S had four-wheel drive fitted to a Turbo chassis and wide body.

GT2   Lightweight version of Turbo body with rear-wheel drive: Power windows, power mirrors, central locking, power seats, sound insulation, and rear seats were deleted. Equipped with plastic fender extensions, adjustable plastic rear wing with air intakes on sides, aluminum doors, aluminum trunk lid, thinner glass for side and rear windows. MOMO steering wheel w/o airbag. Lightweight sport seats with fixed backrest. Limited-slip differential and ABD standard equipment. Speedline wheels: 9Jx18 front, 11Jx18 rear. Tires were 235/40ZR18 front, 285/35ZR18 rear. Weight: 2,845 pounds. Options include Clubsport package (rollcage, six-point harness, racing seats, fire extinguisher, battery cut-off switch), dual airbags and standard steering wheel, air conditioning, and radio.

Carrera 4S   Turbo Look body and chassis with four-wheel drive and normally aspirated engine. Moveable spoiler fitted instead of Turbo rear wing. Turbo brakes and Turbo wheels and tires.

V Program – Produced from August 1996 to July 1997

Model (993)	Chassis Serial No.	Engine Serial No.	Produced
Carrera	WPOZZZ99ZVS310001–5794	63T00001–on (M64/21)	5,794
Carrera Targa	WPOZZZ99ZVS380001–1276		1,276
Carrera Cabriolet	WPOZZZ99ZVS330001–1679		1,679
Carrera U.S./Canada	WPOAA299CVS320001–4972	64T00001–on (M64/23)	4,972
Carrera Targa U.S./Canada	WPOBA299CVS385001–5567		567
Carrera Cabrio U.S./Canada	WPOCA299CVS340001–2157		2,157
Turbo	WPOZZZ99ZVS370001–0972	61T00001–on (M64/60)	972
Turbo U.S./Canada	WPOAA299CVS375001–6046		1,046

Serial number code changes were as follows: The 10th digit changed to "V" to designate the 1997 model year.

Engines
Type M64/21 engine fitted to RoW 993 models
Type M64/22 engine fitted to RoW 993 models with Tiptronic
Type M64/23 fitted to U.S. 993 models
    Designated Type M64/24 fitted to U.S. 993 models with Tiptronic
Type M64/60 fitted to all Turbo models

Transmissions
Type G50/20 six-speed manual transmission for U.S. 993 models
Type G50/21 six-speed manual for RoW 993 models
Type A50/04 four-speed Tiptronic S for RoW 993 models
Type A50/05 four-speed Tiptronic S for U.S. 993 models
Type G64/51 six-speed manual fitted to Turbo models

Convertible top colors for 1997 were Black, Classic Gray, Dark Blue, and Chestnut.

Exterior
Standard Colors

Color Code	Color
Q1	Pastel Yellow
G1	Guards Red
J1	Blue Turquoise
A1	Black
Z1	Glacier White

Special Order Colors

Color Code	Color
X1	Arctic Silver Metallic
Z8	Black Metallic
E1	Ocean Blue Metallic
H8	Arena Red Metallic
F1	Zenith Blue Metallic
To sample	Solid or Metallic colors

Interior
Leatherette (vinyl) standard:
 Chestnut Brown, Midnight Blue, Black, Classic Gray, or Cashmire Beige
Leather, optional:
 Chestnut Brown, Midnight Blue, Black, Classic Gray, or Cashmire Beige
Special order:
 Rubicon Gray, Boxster Red, or Nephrite

Custom leather available to sample.

"Porsche" cloth:

Chestnut Brown, Midnight Blue, Black, Classic Gray, or Cashmire Beige

Carpets:

Classic Gray, Midnight Blue, Black, Cashmire Beige, or Chestnut Brown

Special order:

Boxster Red, Nephrite, or Rubicon Gray

Cabriolet top:

Black, Chestnut Brown, Dark Blue, or Classic Gray

Options

MP08	Active limited-slip differential
MP14	Heated seats
MP15	Full power seats, left & right
MP31	Sport suspension, two 17-inch wheels
M058	Bumpers with impact absorbers
M224	Active brake differential
M333	Blaupunkt Paris RCR42 radio/cassette
M334	Blaupunkt Bremen RCM42 radio/cassette
M383	Sport seat, left
M387	Sport seat, right
M398	17-inch Cup Design wheels
M425	Rear wiper (coupe only)
M437	Full power seat, left only
M438	Full power seat, right only
M454	Cruise control
M490	Radio loudspeaker system
M498	Delete external model designation
M545	92-liter fuel tank
M551	Wind deflector, Cabriolet
M567	Graduated tint windshield
M573	Automatic air conditioning
M586	Lumbar support in seat, left
M513	Lumbar support in seat, right
M613	Porsche telephone, Motorola D-Netz (Germany only)
M650	Power sunroof
M659	On-board computer, standard w/Tiptronic
M692	CD changer (only w/M334 or M490)
M693	Blaupunkt London RMD42 radio/CD player
Carrera S	Turbo Look body similar to Carrera 4S but with two-wheel drive

Chapter 11

1998–1999, 1996 Carrera

1998: The new 996 debuted in coupe form as a 1998 model in Germany. U.S. models were unveiled in spring 1998 as 1999 models.

The flat six-cylinder engine was water-cooled for the first time. The new engine was 3.4 liters with four valves per cylinder, twin plug heads, and dual overhead camshafts. Variocam variable valve timing and a new version of the Varioram intake system were also features of the new engine.

Manual transmission was a new six-speed built by Getrag; the Tiptronic was upgraded to a five-speed. Cable-actuated shift linkage replaced the 993's rod-actuated linkage.

The wheelbase was increased 3.2 inches to 92.6 inches total. The MacPherson strut front suspension was shared with the Boxster and featured aluminum alloy control arms and coil springs over twin- sleeve gas pressure shocks. The rack-and-pinion steering was mounted ahead of the front axle and power assisted. The rear suspension was an independent multi-link design with coil-over single-sleeve gas pressure shocks. Brakes featured power-assisted, dual circuits with four-piston aluminum alloy monoblock fixed calipers. Brake discs were ventilated and cross-drilled, 318-millimeters (12.53 inches) in front, and 299-millimeters (11.78 inches) in the rear.

Standard wheels for the new 911 were cast alloy 7Jx17 in front and 9Jx17 in rear. Tires supplied were 205/50ZR and 255/40ZR, respectively. Optional wheels were 7.5Jx18 with 225/40ZR tires in front and 10Jx18 with 265/35ZR tires at the rear. Dual front and side airbags were standard.

1999: Coupe and Cabriolet in two- and four-wheel drive were available in the United States. A special GT3 model debuted but was not available in the United States. Prepped for racing, the car weighed 2,976 pounds—66 pounds heavier than a stock 996. This was due primarily to strengthening the bodywork and a heavier racing engine. The engine was 3.6 liters, derived from the GT1 engine, and rated at 360 horsepower @ 7,200 rpm. The car came equipped with an adjustable racing suspension. The special body kit included a front spoiler, side sills, and dual plane rear wing. The interior featured sport seats, but other interior trim was deleted. Air conditioning and stereo were available as no-cost options. The Clubsport version was available with a bolted-in rollcage.

U.S. prices: Carrera 2 coupe, $65,030; Cabriolet, $74,460. Carrera 4 coupe, $70,480; Cabriolet, $79,920.

Dimensions	1999 996
Wheelbase:	92.6 inches
Height:	51.4 inches
Width:	69.5 inches
Weight: C2	2910 pounds
Fuel tank capacity	16.9 gallons

W Program – Produced from August 1997 to July 1998

Model (993)	Chassis Serial No.	Engine Serial No.	Produced
Carrera	WPOZZZ99ZWS310001–0841	63T00001–on (M64/21)	780
Carrera Targa	WPOZZZ99ZWS380001–0272		212
Carrera Cabriolet	WPOZZZ99ZWS330001–0198		138
Carrera U.S./Canada	WPOAA299CWS320001–1353	64W00001–on (M64/23)	1,292
Carrera Targa U.S./Canada	WPOBA299CWS385001–5182	64W50001–on (M64/24)	122
Carrera Cabrio U.S./Canada	WPOCA299CWS340001–1263		1,201
Turbo	WPOZZZ99ZWS370001–0801	61W00001–on (M64/60)	739
Carrera Cup	WPOZZZ99ZWS398001–8030	63W80001–on (M64/70)	30
GT2	WPOZZZ99ZWS392001–2081		21

Model (996)	Chassis Serial No.	Engine Serial No.	Produced
Carrera	WPOZZZ99ZWS600001–8296	66W00001–on (M96/01)	8,223
Carrera Cabriolet	WPOZZZ99ZWS640001–0999		937
Carrera Mexico	WPOZZZ99ZWS620001–0151		32
Carrera Cabriolet Mexico	WPOZZZ99ZWS650001–0074		14
Carrera Brazil	WPOZZZ99ZWS629801–9812		12
Carrera Cabriolet Brazil	WPOZZZ99ZWS659801–9801		1
Carerra Cup	WPOZZZ99ZWS698001–8029	63W20001–on (M96/75)	29

Serial number code changes were as follows: The tenth digit changed to "W" to designate the 1998 model year.

The new model designation of 996 was shown by the seventh and eighth digits, which remained as "99," and the twelfth, which became "6."

Engines

Type M64/21 engine fitted to RoW 993 models. Designated Type M64/22 engine fitted to RoW 993 models with Tiptronic

Type M64/23 fitted to U.S. 993 models

Designated Type M64/24 fitted to U.S. 993 models with Tiptronic

Type M64/60 fitted to all Turbo models

Type M 96/01 fitted to 996 models

96-millimeter bore x 78-millimeter stroke

3.4-liters, 3,387 cc

Liquid-cooled

Four valves per cylinder, four overhead camshafts

Bosch Motronic 5.2.2 engine management system

Compression ratio is 11.3:1

Variocam, variable valve-timing system

Varioram, variable intake system

300 horsepower @ 6,800 rpm

258 foot-pounds torque @ 4,600 rpm

Carrera Cup GT3 (996)

3.6-liter Type M96/75

Liquid-cooled

360 horsepower @ 7,200 rpm

The 996 model was the first 911 to have a liquid-cooled engine. This "New 911" debuted in 1998 as a coupe.

Transmissions

Type G50/20 six-speed manual transmission for U.S. 993 models
Type G50/21 six-speed manual for RoW 993 models
Type A50/04 four-speed Tiptronic S for RoW 993 models
Type A50/05 four-speed Tiptronic S for U.S. and Taiwan 993 models
Type G64/51 six-speed manual fitted to Turbo models
Type G64/52 six-speed manual fitted to Turbo models, Taiwan
Type G96/00 six-speed manual for 996 models
    Getrag redesigned for added power and torque
    Cable-actuated shifter
Type A96/00 five-speed Tiptronic optional on 996 models
    ZF-built

Exterior
Standard Colors

Color Code	Color
Q1	Pastel Yellow
G1	Guards Red
J1	Blue Turquoise
A1	Black
Z1	Glacier White

Special Order Colors

Color Code	Color
X1	Arctic Silver Metallic
Z8	Black Metallic
E1	Ocean Blue Metallic
H8	Arena Red Metallic

With 282 horsepower and all-wheel drive, the 996 model Carrera 4 Cabriolet was the most sophisticated convertible available when it was released in 1999.

Color Code	**Color** *(continued)*
F1	Zenith Blue Metallic
To sample	Solid or Metallic colors

Interior

Leatherette (vinyl) standard:
> Chestnut Brown, Midnight Blue, Black, Classic Gray, or Cashmire Beige

Leather, optional:
> Chestnut Brown, Midnight Blue, Black, Classic Gray, or Cashmire Beige

Special order:
> Rubicon Gray, Boxster Red, or Nephrite

Custom leather available to sample.

"Porsche" cloth:
> Chestnut Brown, Midnight Blue, Black, Classic Gray, or Cashmire Beige

Carpets:
> Classic Gray, Midnight Blue, Black, Cashmire Beige, or Chestnut Brown

Special order:
> Boxster Red, Nephrite, or Rubicon Gray

Cabriolet top:
> Black, Chestnut Brown, Dark Blue, or Classic Gray

Options

Same as previous year for 993 models
See 1999 model year for 996 listing

X Program – Produced from August 1998 to July 1999

Model (996)	Chassis Serial No.	Engine Serial No.	Produced
Carrera	WPOZZZ99ZXS600001–8210	66X00001–on (M96/01)	8,156
Carrera Cabriolet	WPOZZZ99ZXS640001–6131	68X00001–on (M96/02)	6,056
Carrera U.S./Canada/Mexico	WPOAA299CXS620001–		7260
Carrera Cabrio U.S./Canada/Mexico	WPOCA299CXS650001–6615		6,482
Carrera Brazil	WPOZZZ99ZXS629801–9802		2
Carrera Cabriolet Brazil	WPOZZZ99ZXS659801–9801		1
Carerra Cup	WPOZZZ99ZXS698001–8081	63X20001–on (M96/75)	81

Serial number code changes were as follows: The 10th digit changed to "X" to designate the 1999 model year.

Engines
Type M96/01 fitted to 996 models
> 96-millimeter bore x 78-millimeter stroke
> 3.4-liters, 3,387 cc
> Liquid-cooled
> Four valves per cylinder, four overhead camshafts
> Bosch Motronic 5.2.2 engine management system
> Compression ratio is 11.3:1
> Variocam, variable valve-timing system
> Varioram, variable intake system
> 300 horsepower @ 6,800 rpm
> 258 foot-pounds torque @ 4,600 rpm

Type M96/02 fitted to cars with e-gas (throttle by wire)

Transmissions
Type G96/00 six-speed manual for 996 models with two-wheel drive
Type G96/30 six-speed manual for 996 models with four-wheel drive
Type A96/00 five-speed Tiptronic optional on 996 two-wheel-drive models
Type A96/30 five-speed Tiptronic optional on 996 four-wheel-drive models

Exterior
Standard Colors

Color Code	Color
Q1	Pastel Yellow
G1	Guards Red
A1	Black
Z1	Glacier White

Optional Colors

Color Code	Color
X1	Arctic Silver Metallic
Z8	Black Metallic
E1	Ocean Blue Metallic
H8	Arena Red Metallic
F1	Zenith Blue Metallic
J3	Ocean Jade Metallic
K3	Vesuvio Metallic
T1	Mirage Metallic
To sample	Solid (98) or Metallic (99)

Optional colors cost $805
Colors to sample cost $4,230 and could add three to six months to
delivery time

Special Order Colors

Color Code	Color
50	Speed Yellow
51	Wimbledon Green Metallic

Color Code	Color *(continued)*
53	Forest Green Metallic
54	Viola Metallic
55	Dark Blue
56	Cobalt Blue Metallic
58	Polar Silver Metallic
59	Slate Gray Metallic
61	Iris Blue Metallic
62	Midnight Blue Metallic

Special order colors cost $3,010 and could add two to four weeks to delivery time.

Interior

Leatherette w/partial leather seats standard ($1,490 cost):
 Space Gray, Metropol Blue, Black, Graphite Gray, or Savanna Beige
Leather, optional (cost $3,215):
 Above colors (includes leather steering wheel, side panels, dash, shift lever boot & knob, handbrake handle, door panels, and armrest/center storage top)
Special order colors (cost $3,655): Boxster Red, or Nephrite
Custom leather available to sample (cost $4,930)
Standard leather, deviating color application ($3,500)
Carpets:
 Space Gray, Metropol Blue, Black, Graphite Gray, or Savanna Beige
Special order:
 Boxster Red, or Nephrite
Cabriolet top:
 Black, Graphite Gray, Metropol Blue, or Space Gray

Options

Code	Option	Cost
M030	Sport suspension	$690
M288	Headlight washers	225
M413	18-inch Turbo Look alloy wheels	1,190
M425	Rear window wiper	335
M436	Three-spoke leather steering wheel w/airbag	255
M446	Wheel caps w/colored Porsche crest; 18-inch only	170
M490	Hi-Fi sound system 10 speakers/amp.	600
M498	Delete model designation	N/C
M513	Lumbar support, passenger side, adjustable	375
M549	Roof rack	390
M571	Carbon air filter, interior	460
M580	Non-smoker Package	N/C
M586	Lumbar support, driver's seat	375
M601	Litronic headlights	1,070
M635	Park assist system	520
M652	Delete sunroof	N/C

Code	Option	Cost
M659	On-board computer	275
M662	PCM navigation system	3,540
M692	Remote six CD-changer	705
M696	AM/FM radio w/CD	345
M982	Soft look leather seats	390
E70	Leather Package: dash, vents, speaker cover, etc.	2,922
E71	Maple Burr Package Light	5,876
E72	Maple Burr Package Dark	5,876
E73	Carbon Package	5,876
FLY	Air transport from factory	4,000
M6A	Black floor mat "PORSCHE"	110
M6E	Space Gray mat	110
M6F	Metropol Blue mat	110
M6J	Nephrite Green mat	110
M6M	Boxster Red mat	110
M6P	Graphite Gray mat	110
M6S	Savanna Beige mat	110
P14	Heated seats	400
P15	Electrically adjustable seats, L&R, driver's memory	1,520
P49	Digital Sound Package (includes M490)	1,175
P77	Leather sport seats	745
VA3	Tourist delivery prep	N/C
X26	Steering all leather	1,311
X28	Light Maple Burr wood steering wheel	1,660
X30	Dark Maple Burr wood steering wheel	1,660
X45	Instrument dials matching interior color	764
X54	Stainless steel exhaust pipes	747
X69	Door sills in carbon embossed w/model insignia	764
X70	Door sills, stainless steel w/model insignia	415
X71	Aluminum painted instrument dials	913
X77	Airbag steering wheel combination of carbon and interior color leather	1,660
X89	Wheel caps w/Porsche crest on painted wheels	291
XAA	Aerokit	7,968
XAD	Rear side GT fins	747
XD3	Rain sensor windshield	581
XD9	Painted wheels, body color	1,342
XE3	Auto dimming rear mirror	432
XEH	Self-dimming inner and outer rearview mirror	697
XJB	Rear center console painted silver	714
XKX	Lower part of instrument panel painted silver	216
XMA	Roofliner, A&B pillars in leather	1,378
XME	Rear center console painted body color	714
XMF	Front console in leather	481
XMJ	Rear center console, carbon	1,594

Code	Option	Cost
XML	Rear center console, lt. wood	1,594
XMP	Leather sun visors, lighted mirror	548
XMZ	Rear center console, leather	1,228
XNB	Rear center console, drk. wood	1,594
XND	Lower instrument panel, body color	216
XNS	Steering column in leather	310
XPA	Three-spoke steering wheel, lthr.	1,511
XPB	Three-spoke steering wheel, lt wood/lthr.	1,843
XPC	Three-spoke steering wheel, dk. wood/lthr.	1,843
XPD	Three-spoke steering wheel, carbon/lthr	1,843
XRB	18-inch Sport Classic wheels/tires	2,656
XRL	18-inch Sport Design wheel	2,656
XSA	Sport seats rear side of backrest painted to match body color	1,461
XSB	Sport seats rear side of backrest covered in leather	1,577
XSC	Porsche crest in headrest	208
XSD	Seat adj. knobs in leather color	797
XTG	Inner rocker panels covered in leather	498
XTJ	Door grip, lt. wood/lthr.	1,145
XTK	Door grip, dk. wood/lthr.	1,145
XTL	Door grip, carbon/lthr.	1,145
XTN	Mirror adj. cover, lthr.	216
XX1	Front floor mats embroidered "Porsche"	415
XX2	Footwell lighting	714
XZD	Dome lamp cover, lthr.	324
Y05	Carbon/aluminum shift knob and brake handle	880
Y06	Lthr./aluminum shift knob and brake handle	880
Y07	Lt. Maple/aluminum shift knob and brake handle	880
Y08	Dk. Maple/aluminum shift knob and brake handle	880
Y29	Aluminum & Chrome Package: X54, X70, X71	1,942
Z108	Upper dash in deviating color	134
Z109	Lower dash in deviating color	75
Z110	Instrument hump in deviating color	136
Z111	Seat insert in deviating color	1,780
Z34	Carpet in deviating color	290
Z48	Front hood w/o Porsche crest	142
Z50	Seatbelts (front & rear) in Guards Red, Speed Yellow, or Riviera Blue	518
Z77	Steering wheel deviating from std. color	91
Z84	Stitching on F/R seats in deviating color	225
Z88	All visible stitching inside car in deviating color (not including seats)	285
Z96	Roofliner in leatherette, deviating color	135

Appendix

Comparative Performance Chart of Various 911 Models through the Years

Model	Engine	0-60 mph	1/4-mile	Top Speed	Source
1965 Coupe	2.0-liter	9.0 sec	16.5 sec	132 mph	*Road & Track*
1967 911S	2.0-liter	8.1 sec	15.7 sec	141 mph	*Road & Track*
1968 911L/Sportomatic	2.0-liter	10.3 sec	17.3 sec	117 mph	*Road & Track*
1970 911S	2.2-liter	7.3 sec	14.9 sec	144 mph	*Road & Track*
1972 911T	2.4-liter	6.9 sec	15.1 sec	N/A	*Car and Driver*
1972 911S	2.4-liter	6.0 sec	14.4 sec	N/A	*Car and Driver*
1973 Carrera RSR	2.7-liter	5.6 sec	13.2 sec	N/A	*Road & Track*
1974 911	2.7-liter	7.9 sec	15.5 sec	130 mph	*Road & Track*
1975 California Carrera	2.7-liter	8.2 sec	16.5 sec	134 mph	*Road & Track*
1975 Turbo	3.0-liter	5.5 sec*	24.2 sec**	152.9 mph	*Automobil Revue* (Swiss)
1976 935 Turbo	2.8-liter	3.3 sec	8.9 sec	150 mph	*Road & Track*
1978 911SC	3.0-liter	6.3 sec	15.3 sec	N/A	*Road & Track*
1979 930 Turbo	3.3-liter	5.3 sec	13.4 sec	160 mph	*Motor*
1993 RS America	3.6-liter	5.4 sec	N/A	162 mph	*Porsche*
1995 Turbo	3.6-liter	3.9 sec	12.5 sec	180 mph	*Road & Track*
1998 993	3.6-liter	5.4 sec	N/A	171 mph	*Porsche*
1999 996	3.4-liter	5.2 sec	N/A	174 mph	*Porsche*

* 0 to 62 mph (100 kph)

** One kilometer distance from standing start.

NOTE: Information for this chart has been compiled from various sources and does not necessarily represent the definitive performance of any of the models listed. Its purpose is to entertain 911 aficionados as much as enlighten them. As a longtime 911 owner, and a fan for a far longer time, it is my way of reminding readers that while I have tried to give you as much information in this book as I could, the best way to learn about the 911 is to drive a few.

Bibliography

Original Porsche 911, Peter Morgan, MBI Publishing Company, 1998

Porsche 911, Forever Young, Tobias Aichele, Motorbuch-Verlag/
Pietsch-Verlag, 1993

Porsche 911 Performance Handbook, Bruce Anderson, MBI
Publishing Company, 1996

Porsche 911 Road Cars, Dennis Adler, MBI Publishing Company, 1998

Porsche 911 R-RS-RSR, John Starkey, Veloce Publishing Plc., 1998

The Porsche 911, Chris Harvey, The Oxford Illustrated Press, 1983

Porsche 911 Story, 6th Edition, Paul Frere, Patrick Stephens,
Limited, 1997

The Porsche Book, Lothar Boschen and Jurgen Barth, Arco
Publishing, Inc., 1977

Porsche, Excellence Was Expected, Karl Ludvigsen, Princeton
Publishing, Inc., 1977

The Porsche Family Tree, Drayton James, Editor, PEA, Porsche
Club of America, 1995